MINDFULNESS AND CHRISTIAN SPIRITUALITY

Making space for God

Tim Stead

First published in Great Britain in 2016

Society for Promoting Christian Knowledge
36 Causton Street
London SW1P 4ST
www.spck.org.uk

British Library Cataloguing-in-Publication Data
A catalogue record for this book is available from the British Library

ISBN 978–0–281–07486–0
eBook ISBN 978–0–281–07487–7

Typeset by Graphicraft Limited, Hong Kong
First printed in Great Britain by Ashford Colour Press
Subsequently digitally printed in Great Britain

eBook by Graphicraft Limited, Hong Kong

Produced on paper from sustainable forests

Did you know that SPCK is a registered charity?

As well as publishing great books by leading Christian authors, we also . . .

. . . make assemblies meaningful and fun for over a million children by running www.assemblies.org.uk, a popular website that provides free assembly scripts for teachers. For many children, school assembly is the only contact they have with Christian faith and culture, and the only time in their week for spiritual reflection.

. . . help prisoners to become confident readers with our easy-to-read stories. Poor literacy is a huge barrier to rehabilitation. Prisoners identify with the believable heroes of our gritty fiction. At the same time, questions at the end of each chapter help them to examine their choices from a moral perspective and to build their reading confidence.

. . . support student ministers overseas in their training through partnerships in the Global South.

Please support these great schemes: visit www.spck.org.uk/support-us to find out more.

Tim Stead graduated with an engineering degree in 1982, has been an ordained Anglican priest for 20 years and is currently Vicar of Holy Trinity, Headington Quarry, Oxford. He is an accredited mindfulness teacher with the Oxford Mindfulness Centre and teaches their eight-week Mindfulness Based Cognitive Therapy (MBCT) course as well as running mindfulness courses and retreats in the parish and for clergy in the diocese.

To our parents, Liz and John – the light and the dark of my early years. I am grateful for both

Contents

———•◆•———

Contents

Foreword

I was driving back to Oxford along the country road from Stratford. It was a sunny spring day, so I was happy to drive in silence. Occasionally, I would pass a sign with a picture of a camera on it. My mind wandered on to thinking about those satnav systems that warn the driver when a speed camera is coming up, and whether it would be right or useful to get one. Soon, my mind was so full of thoughts of traffic cameras that I did not see the *actual* camera until too late.

Thinking *about* something is not the same as really attending to it. As William James said, 'Knowledge *about* things, as distinguished from living or sympathetic acquaintance *with* them, touches only the outer surface of reality.'* Words, whether they are spoken or thought or written, present us with a world of ideas that are so good at representing reality that we unwittingly use them as a stand-in for the actual experience.

Religion is not immune to this. Awareness of a Presence or Power in the universe and the deep silence from which it originates soon gives way to words *about* the experience. We move from poetry to prose, from a glimmer of understanding to the harsher light of dogma, and from a celebration of openness to a perceived need to defend closed positions. We become so preoccupied with finding the meaning of life that we lose touch with the experience of being alive.

Tim Stead's book seeks to redress the balance by showing how we can make space for life and for God. One of the ways

---

* W. James, *A Pluralistic Universe*, 1909, available as an e-book through Google Books. See Joel D. S. Rasmussen, 'Williams James, *A Pluralistic Universe* and the ancient quarrel between philosophy and poetry', in M. Halliwell and J. D. S. Rasmussen, *Williams James and the Transatlantic Conversation*, Oxford: Oxford University Press, 2014, pp. 151–66.

our faith can be brought back to life, he says, is not by believing the right things, but through a practice: the practice of mindfulness.

Mindfulness means *awareness*, a lucid and appreciative 'knowing' what we are doing as we are doing it. Although it is central to the Buddhist tradition, mindful awareness is also found in the Christian contemplative tradition and in any case is not about being a Buddhist, but about being human.

Mindfulness can nourish and renew faith. Tim Stead does not assert this as dogma, but rather by inviting us to see what happens when we train the mind to attend, moment by moment and without harsh judgement, to what is going on in the exterior and interior world. Through regular meditation practice, we find that mindfulness transforms our lives, brings a sense of peace, of having more time, of being less hectic. Mindfulness allows us to turn towards what we fear with greater courage and open-heartedness and to be released for loving action in the world.

But isn't this what Christianity does? What on earth can mindfulness add to the rich spiritual resources within Christianity already? This is a good question. There *is* an extraordinary breadth and depth of Christian spiritual practice over many centuries, and much of it has at its core the cultivation of loving awareness. We need to be careful, however, that our assertion of the spiritual riches within our tradition does not arise from a subtle sense that we (inside the Church) have already got all the answers and simply need people (outside the Church) to rouse themselves and catch up – to 'get with the programme'. It's all too easy to think that if only people would read this or that spiritual master or come to the series of talks or services going on in our local cathedral or church, they would soon see the relevance of the contemplative life within Christianity.

A Cyrus moment?

Reformation from within the Christian Church may be possible, but it seems that, in mindfulness, we are being offered something, the whole advantage of which is that it comes from 'outside'. This may be a *Cyrus moment* for Christians, and if this is true, it must not be ignored. What is a Cyrus moment? The reference comes from the writings of the prophet Isaiah (chapter 45). Speaking to the children of Israel in exile in Babylon, Isaiah said that freedom would be accomplished through his 'anointed, Cyrus'. The word 'anointed', normally reserved for Jewish kings, was being extended to a Persian king. What's more, this king knew nothing about the Hebrew people's God: 'I call you by your name,... though you do not know me' (v. 4). The message of Isaiah to his people was to trust that God could use something or someone from outside to end their exile and bring them home.

If we insist that all we need is already to be found within Christianity, we may be in danger of missing the moment when something God-inspired, from outside our own tradition, offers us a transformative liberation that we were desperate for, but couldn't find from within it.

What if, instead, we followed Tim Stead's wise advice and opened ourselves to the riches of this other source of wisdom, a source of exquisite subtlety and beauty? This is not about reading books about Buddhism, which might simply be more words. Rather it is about setting time aside for regular practice. Then we might rediscover the Ground of all Being, and that a deep and God-given stillness and peace was available to us even in the midst of the brokenness and chaos of our lives.

Tim Stead's book is addressed to his own Christian tradition, but people of other faiths or none will find it offers enormous potential, for it points towards a universal source of healing.

You can read this book in a few days; but take it to heart, and it will last a lifetime.

Mark Williams
Emeritus Professor of Clinical Psychology
Honorary Canon of Christ Church Cathedral, Oxford

Thanks

———•◦•———

With many thanks to those who have supported me through my own mindfulness training, especially Marie Johansson, Christina Surawy and Chris Cullen. Also to Mark Williams for his valuable comments and suggestions for the book and for his Foreword. And finally, to Anne Tarassenko and David Harper for reading my first draft, and to Susie my wife and writing partner and my children for regularly reminding me that I am not yet very mindful!

Introduction: Making space for God

'What – another book about mindfulness?!' You may have noticed how books on mindfulness are multiplying like coat hangers in a wardrobe. There is 'mindfulness and this', 'mindfulness and that' and soon, probably, 'mindfulness and the other'. It is clearly the big new thing and therefore probably time to get cynical about it and start wearing the 'I don't do mindfulness' T-shirt.

However, there is very little on mindfulness and Christianity. This seems to me somewhat curious as there are so many overlaps, and something that is the big new thing surely ought to have a Christian response.

I wonder whether there are two reasons for this. One might be that we feel we already have two millennia and more of spiritual tradition behind us and so perhaps this is just 'spirituality' for those who don't belong to any faith. In other words, we don't really need it. And the other is that we have heard that mindfulness has its roots in Buddhism. Now this could be good or bad depending on your point of view, but it is still a 'competing' religion, isn't it, and surely I should be looking to my own faith for my spiritual practices?

Well, all this may be true – or true enough. But there are other questions that may still linger in the mind:

- Could it be that Christianity is still learning?
- Are we open to insights of other faith traditions?
- Is there more of our own tradition that remains generally unexplored?
- Are we open to the insights of science?
- Are we up for a further stage in the adventure of Christian faith and spirituality?

If the answer to any or all of these questions in your own mind is 'yes' – even a qualified 'yes' – then this book may be worth reading.

But first, let me say something about the approach of this book, beginning with what it is not. It is not a textbook on mindfulness, nor is it a mindfulness course. Plenty of these have already been written and are definitely worth turning to if you want to explore mindfulness for yourself in its own right. (A list of good books and where to find a course can be found at the back of this book.) Neither is this a theological treatise. Rather, it seeks to ask the question: 'What might mindfulness have to offer Christianity?' I could have chosen to have a go at answering the question the other way round: 'What does Christianity think of mindfulness?', but actually the former question seems much more interesting and full of possibilities – and perhaps somewhat humbler. So, although I will take time to say something of what mindfulness is and what is beneficial about it in Part 1, I am assuming that it is accepted that it is basically a good thing. Essentially, as psychologists are suggesting, this is about having a healthy mind, just as physical exercise and a good diet lead to a healthy body. But I want to go further than this and suggest that mindfulness might have a part to play in helping Christians to respond to the call of Christ in our lives.

I have always had two burning questions when I have thought about my faith:

1 Does it make sense?
2 Does it make a difference?

As far as the first question is concerned, apart from my earliest days as a Christian, when I simply took everything as read, I have always been someone who has wrestled with belief and the statements of faith that we proclaim. There have been times when I have simply wanted to say, 'I can't believe that.' But in the end, that has seemed a bit presumptuous and anyway it doesn't really lead me anywhere. So, what has seemed a more interesting question has been, 'I wonder what we really mean by saying that?' – about God, about Jesus, or whatever. This keeps the question open and the quest alive. So Part 2 will take time to reflect on what mindfulness might have to offer in terms of what and how we believe.

The second question has been almost more pressing for me. I know that Christian faith offers comfort, inspiration and a sense of purpose, but can it actually change anything? Or are we simply forever 'moving the deckchairs around on the *Titanic*' – offering 'opium for the people' because basically the news is bad and always will be? I deeply want a faith and a spiritual practice that works – that can make a difference to my life and really change things for the better in all of our lives. Added to this is that many of us are acutely aware of a kind of faith that lays down very clearly what we ought to be or what we ought to do, but feel a constant sense of failure in the extent to which we have actually been able to live up to such expectations. And that is just the reasonably humble and self-aware ones! My New Testament teacher at theological college used to remark on how people would say to him that they weren't really Christian but they did live by the Sermon on the Mount. To which he would reply, 'Have you *read* the Sermon on the Mount?!' If they had, he would surmise, they would have realized that the ideal is, in fact, impossible. For those who have realized this, though, it may not be quite enough simply to accept God's forgiveness for our failure. We do genuinely want to find ways of respond-ing, growing, moving towards this ideal, however slowly. So, does our Christian faith work? Does it make any difference? Mindfulness, for me, also has a part to play in enabling our faith to work for us, and in Part 3 I will suggest some ways in which this might be true.

Part 1, though, addresses the question, 'What is mindfulness?' This is not a mini course, but I hope it will provide a basic understanding of mindfulness itself. I approach it in three ways: first, by telling the story of the development of mindfulness in its clinical and academic contexts; second, by reflecting on mindfulness in the Christian tradition; and finally, by reflecting on mindfulness from the perspective of my own faith journey.

However, an important point to note at every stage is that mindfulness is only truly appreciated at an experiential level. Because of this, practical exercises are interspersed throughout the book, which you are welcome to have a go at. These are no more than tasters, but will, I hope, give balance to the mainly reflective material.

Finally, a word on the subtitle of the book: *Making Space for God*. We cannot save ourselves. We cannot even heal ourselves. Christians believe that only God, in Christ, is our Saviour and healer. But there is something we can do – and need to do – and that is to make space for God to come to us. We can choose to open ourselves up and invite the work of grace into our lives. This may be familiar language but still it raises the question: 'But how do we do this opening up and inviting in?' It is my suggestion that mindfulness offers us a way of opening up, inviting in – making space for God.

Part 1

WHAT IS MINDFULNESS?

1

Mindfulness in its clinical and mainstream contexts

————◆•◆•◆————

If you already know the basics of mindfulness, or have even completed a course, then you might want to skip this chapter (although, equally, you might just be interested in my own slant). But for those who don't have a basic knowledge, this chapter covers how mindfulness has emerged in the past 40 years (first in clinical settings and lately in all sorts of mainstream contexts), what it actually is, how it is taught generally and how I have been teaching it in the parish context.

History

The story goes back to the 1970s when Jon Kabat-Zinn, with a PhD in molecular biology from the Massachusetts Institute of Technology, began to develop a meditation-based programme to help support people suffering from chronic pain. Kabat-Zinn had been introduced to the practice of meditation a few years earlier and was influenced by the world-renowned Buddhist teacher Thich Nhat Hahn, among others. Kabat-Zinn was born Jewish but suggests that his world view was more strongly formed by the science and art learned from his parents than by any religious context. Similarly, when he discovered meditation it was not the religious aspects that drew him but the health value of the practices. He does not identify as a Buddhist any more than he identifies as a Jew, but rather has explored all that he has been exposed to in relation to his own scientific

3

context. So, when he began to realize that the practices he was engaging with might have some significant health benefits, he developed an eight-week programme that later became known as Mindfulness Based Stress Reduction (MBSR). He offered this in the University of Massachusetts Medical School and demonstrated through controlled tests that the course could significantly reduce anxiety and stress in patients, and in particular help people to find an alternative way of managing chronic pain. The programme has been running ever since and is now available all over the world.

There is a very moving video, *Healing and the Mind* (available on YouTube[1]), of Kabat-Zinn teaching a class of people with severe, untreatable chronic pain of all kinds, showing how the practices helped to transform the lives of the participants. These patients had already exhausted all the possibilities provided by conventional medicine for elimination of their pain. Mindfulness practice was *not* being offered as another way to eliminate pain, however. Instead, MBSR taught the participants a new way of *relating* to their pain. This reduced the considerable degree of stress with which most people usually respond to pain, and this, in turn, reduced the perceived experience of pain to the extent that many could take fewer painkillers, and often either go back to work or engage in activities they had previously withdrawn from. But the most striking thing about the video, which seems to me particularly important to note, is the compassion that seems to flow from the teacher. Kabat-Zinn appears genuinely to care for his patients in a heartfelt way. If, as Kabat-Zinn says, this is really all science, then it was science with a difference, because it included as a necessary fundamental element the lived-out experience of love.

Fast-forward to the 1990s and we find a group of cognitive behaviour therapists on two continents reflecting on the effectiveness of their treatment for long-term sufferers of depression. Recall that, up until then, psychiatry and psychology had been focusing on how to treat depression once people were already in the midst of an episode. Cognitive behaviour therapy (CBT) had been shown to have been a very successful treatment since the 1970s, but what Mark Williams, John Teasdale and Zindel Segal were finding was that a major problem for people with depression was that it keeps coming back – it is a 'recurrent' problem – especially for those treated with antidepressant medication. These psychologists thought that such recurrence might be due to the fact that, for many who have suffered past episodes of depression, a new episode is more and more easily triggered. For these people, any small initial low mood could activate a whole chain of associations, forming into negative thought patterns that then compound and deepen the mood into a full-blown depression. CBT was known to help reduce recurrence, but no one knew how it had its therapeutic effects. Segal, Williams and Teasdale suggested that CBT had implicitly been teaching people a way to step back from the vicious cycle of their thoughts rather than constantly getting caught up in them. If this is how successful treatment actually worked, could the same skill be taught to those who were known to be vulnerable to future depression even when they were well? But how could this be achieved? It was at this time that they became aware of Kabat-Zinn's work in Massachusetts, through his publications, which had begun to emerge in the early 1990s.

So, the CBT experts travelled to America, took part in the MBSR programme and came to realize that this could be the missing piece to their own jigsaw. After one or two false starts, most notably making the mistake of thinking that mindfulness could be taught by people who were not actually practising it themselves, they developed an eight-week programme called Mindfulness Based Cognitive Therapy (MBCT). This was based heavily on the MBSR programme but was adapted to focus on the needs of long-term sufferers of depression. CBT was still in there, as it had been shown to be so effective in the past, but it was now 'front-loaded' with mindfulness. Essentially, participants were shown a way of disengaging from their negative thought processes in order to create space around them before then employing some gentle CBT techniques.

The initial results were dramatic. Compared to control groups who continued with treatment as normal (that is, continuing with whatever their usual treatment might be, including going back to medication if they needed to), those who took part in the MBCT programme showed a reduction in episodes of relapse by up to 50 per cent. And it seems to be reduction in relapse for chronic sufferers that is the key achievement. It is generally advised that sufferers of depression take part in an MBCT programme, if possible while they are feeling well. This is partly because the programme is quite demanding in itself and partly because but what it teaches is the skills needed to avoid relapse. Once again it is important to note that compassion is built into the way the programme is taught. Those who have developed the course have been motivated over the decades by their sense of compassion and have realized that this is a key part of the healing process. A final point to note is that, partly because of these initial results and partly because of the unit costs involved (mindfulness can be taught to a group of up to 25 people at a time), NICE (the national body that advises the NHS) were fairly quickly persuaded to back it. You can now be referred by your GP to a mindfulness course, paid for by the NHS.

A definition

So, an extraordinary success story! Mindfulness is a good thing, as declared by psychologists, neuroscientists and health professionals. But what actually is it and how is it taught?

First, a definition: mindfulness can be described as being *more fully aware of your own experience in the present moment in a non-judgemental way*. There are four vital strands to this definition: awareness, experience, the present moment, and non-judgement; all are key parts of what mindfulness is. It may sound very simple or even naive to suggest that bringing mindful awareness to things would have any significant effect on the practitioner, but notice how each of these four aspects is counterintuitive – against the grain of much of our regular 'default' brain activity – and therefore needs a great deal of practice to achieve; and that each aspect plays a significant role in reducing anxiety and living more freely, which consequently seems to have such an effect on many other aspects of our health.

The emphasis on awareness is intended to be offered as a powerful antidote to the automatic way our brains tend to work most of the time. In mindfulness training we refer to this as 'autopilot'. It is important that our brains are able to act automatically (or unconsciously) much of the time, so that we do not have to keep sending a message to our hearts every second to carry on beating, or consider whether we should jump out of the way of an oncoming bus. But much of our unconscious brain activity can be useless at best and dangerous at worst, so the constant practice of bringing awareness to what is going on in our minds can be a very powerful tool. Awareness, as we shall explore later, leads to greater choice in how we use our minds.

The emphasis on our own experience is intended to counteract the brain's tendency to overanalyse. Analysis is, again, an important brain function, as many problems can be solved in this way, but not all. Crucially, very often these exceptions are not emotional or psychological ones. Whatever the case, the art of drawing closer to what it is we are actually experiencing can be an important part of the healing process, especially when analysis may be being used (even inadvertently) only as a means to move away from our experiences.

Emphasis on the present moment is also a key tool for those of us who can spend too much of our time living either in the past or in the future: worrying, replaying or even over-celebrating what has happened, or planning what is about to happen, while never fully appreciating what is right here in

7

front of us. Too much focus on past or future is associated with build-up of stress.

Finally, bringing a non-judging attitude is also key if we are to counter the human tendency to repress those things of which we are ashamed or embarrassed. Once aspects of ourselves are repressed they are less available for healing of any sort. Only when some part of ourselves is fully present in a non-judging atmosphere (akin, you might say, to that created by a good psychotherapist – or even better, God!) can that aspect be more fully understood and be in some way healed.

But why not try this little exercise, if you have never done anything like it before, which illustrates through actual experience what mindfulness is.

The raisin practice

This exercise has become a classic in the teaching of mindfulness. It doesn't have to be done with a raisin; but raisins do seem to work very well.

So, find a few moments to yourself, read through these instructions and then see if you can follow them as best you can.

1 Take one raisin and place it on the palm of your hand. You are going to eat it at some point, but not yet!
2 First, take time simply to see the raisin sitting there on your hand and explore all the visual aspects of this raisin. I know you know it is a raisin and you have seen many before, but you have never seen this one, never at this point in time and never in precisely your current state of mind. So, see if you can see this raisin as though you have never seen one before and you just want to experience it as fully as possible. See the smoothness and the rough patches; the various shades of colour; the way the light plays on the surface; can you see any shadows, etc.

3 Then, when you feel ready, pick the raisin up between your thumb and forefinger and begin to explore its texture and how it feels to the touch. Perhaps roll it around between your fingers and see how the texture changes over time or as it warms up.

4 Next explore its smell by bringing it up to your nose. What do you notice? If you have a cold there may be no smell! If so, then notice simply the absence of smell; but if there is smell, allow yourself to become aware of it for a few moments. Smell is often complex, and there may be more than one kind of aroma around, including, of course, the smell of your own fingers.

5 Now place the raisin on your tongue. Don't chew or swallow yet, if you can manage it, but explore the sensations in the mouth caused by having a raisin on the tongue. You might even move it around to see how other parts of the mouth respond to the introduction of this raisin.

6 Now, when you feel ready, bite into the raisin and notice the flavours that are released, and, again, how the different parts of the mouth respond to these flavours. Where are the flavours most noticeable? Where else are they apparent?

7 Finally, but only when you have decided to, swallow the raisin. But let the practice not end there; stay with your attention and notice all the after-effects on your mouth, throat and body of having swallowed the raisin.

When we teach mindfulness in classes, after this practice we simply invite participants to say something of what they experienced, or noticed in their own experience, during the practice. The array of responses is astonishing and rather wonderful. All we have done is eat a raisin, but people express a wide range of things about a raisin they had never noticed before, and all sorts of thoughts that popped up in their minds in response to what the raisin had triggered. One participant travelled (in her mind) all the way down to the south coast of England and was in her mother's kitchen at Christmas while the Christmas pudding was being prepared. And all I had asked her to do was to eat a single raisin!

Your experience may be different: boredom, irritation, dislike of raisins, self-conscious thoughts about what on earth you are doing when you thought you were going to learn about some new life-changing spirituality! All these may be present. But it doesn't matter *what* we experience or notice, only that we notice it.

How wonderful, then, to go about life in this way: fully awake to the myriad different experiences that are going on around and within us all the time; delighting in things we had never noticed before – the subtle colours, aromas and textures of all we encounter; even waking up fully to the thought processes that are constantly going on in our minds. However, I have only just begun to describe a process. It may sound simple but actually it is very difficult – which is why we practise, practise and practise. Much is said about the practices, but it is the results of being more mindfully aware that we are seeking. Mindfulness has been shown to have many health benefits; and, I will argue, it has huge benefits for the Christian.

Teaching mindfulness

Finally, how is mindfulness taught? This is, for me, part of the genius of what mindfulness might have to offer the churches. Compare, for instance, how you learned to pray. My own experience, even as one who has been quite proactive in seeking to learn spiritual practice over the decades, has been piecemeal at best. There are any number of excellent books, from the greats to the popularizers, and I find that I have learned a bit from here and a bit from there over a long period of searching, but often there is no one on hand to help me when I get stuck. So, what about your average churchgoer, who might ask, as Jesus' disciples once asked, 'How do I pray?' Well, there are books on prayer and courses about prayer on offer, and even the help of a spiritual director if you are really keen, but where is the course that can simply take you through the basics and get you going? Mindfulness does have such a course; in various forms, yes, but all drawing from the same well and all equipping you with the basics, from where you can continue to explore and develop for the rest of your life.

Before describing the course I teach, I want to note one further development in the mindfulness story. Not very long after it was discovered that mindfulness was effective for people suffering from serious clinical conditions, it began to be realized that it could also be of value for all of us, whether we are struggling with milder forms of stress and anxiety, wanting to find a sense of focus in a high-pressure, high-achieving career, or simply wanting to live a fuller and healthier life.

Jon Kabat-Zinn had already written a number of books for the general reader, but in 2011, Mark Williams, together with his writing partner, Danny Penman, published *Mindfulness: A Practical Guide to Finding Peace in a Frantic World*.[2] In this book they presented an eight-week course that could be followed by the reader at home, which had a less specific focus. It was designed not for those with chronic pain or depression, but to respond to the much wider set of aspirations of people living ordinary everyday lives.

The course I teach is based on this book. The broad description below, though common to all the courses, comes from my experience of teaching with this more general book.

Let us start with two key principles.

First, there was an early recognition that mindfulness could only be taught in a mindful way. A bit like with God really; you can teach *about* mindfulness and your hearers (if they don't get bored) will acquire an intellectual knowledge that is almost entirely useless to them – because what they really need is to *experience* mindfulness for themselves. Teaching mindfulness in an experiential way involves inviting the participants to try

11

out the mindfulness practices for themselves, either in class or at home and then to reflect on what they experienced while trying the practice. The aim is not to achieve any particular experience but to develop the skill of noticing what happens in our experience. So the teacher becomes an enabler of experience rather than an imparter of knowledge. It is very common that members of the group will, especially in the early stages, feel despondent that they have not achieved what was required. But the response of the teacher will always be to place the main emphasis on simply noticing what did happen rather than getting frustrated with what didn't. As mentioned earlier, the skill being learned is, in many ways, counterintuitive – we have been brought up with the expectation that we need to reach targets and goals, but here, rather wonderfully, it is different. We are learning to notice what is actually happening, in a non-judgemental way, so that we might come to know the experience more deeply. From this point all else follows.

The second key principle, as noted already from the MBSR and MBCT programmes, is compassion. At every stage the atmosphere we seek to create is one of openness and non-judging compassion. Initially we simply seek to model it; later on, in the course from Williams and Penman's *Frantic World* book, we actually teach it in a particular way. We are hoping that people will learn to be honest and open about their own experiences, and this will only happen if people feel that their teacher is basically on their side and cares deeply about their struggles.

So, against the background of enabling experience in an atmosphere of compassion, the course works through a number of different but related mindfulness practices. Each week there is a new practice, which participants are invited to try at home on six days out of seven, with the help of a guiding CD (which comes with *Frantic World*), and then come back the next week to reflect on the experience.

There are three types of the main formal practices. They often overlap but we gradually move through the three types over the eight weeks. I call these three types 'focus', 'awareness' and 'kindness'.

The focus practices are the starting point and the bedrock of all that follows. First we need a focus – an anchor, or if you like a place to 'stand' from which we can become aware of what is going on in our ever-changing experience. The focus could be anything that stays still; however, in mindfulness we tend for a number of reasons to use the body as our starting point in bringing focus. So one of the basic practices involves developing the ability to direct the mind's attention to various parts of the body in turn. This is called the 'body scan'. Another related practice is to see if it is possible to bring your attention to your own breathing – and keep it there! The first thing most of us find is that it is not possible, or at least not for long. And when I say not for long, for some of us it can often be only a few seconds! So, the first thing we discover in mindfulness is how active the mind is – indeed, how it has a 'mind of its own'. You can be at the end of a long stream of thought about the day's events or plans for tomorrow before you even realize it. The moment you become aware of this, though, you are invited to congratulate yourself for 'waking up' and then simply to return to the focus, whether it is the breath or the body.

This can be such a frustrating phase, as all we seem to be discovering is how little ability to focus we have. And added to this, we are annoyingly assured, there is nothing we can do about this except keep noticing when we have drifted off. Gritting our teeth with the determination to do better this time just doesn't seem to work. And when people have asked me whether I have got better at focusing for longer periods of time over the years, I am afraid I have to answer: not really! I think I have got better at 'waking up', though, and am definitely better at becoming aware during the day, but I don't feel I have got any 'better' at meditating; which, thankfully, is not actually the aim. The aim is to become more mindful in daily life.

The focus practice

To get the basic idea of this kind of practice you could try it for yourself now – this could take as little as five minutes. When you have finished reading the instructions, put the book to one side.

Sit up straight but in a relaxed way, close your eyes if you feel comfortable with that, and deliberately bring your attention to noticing your own breathing, focusing on the part of the body that seems most apparent to you as the breath moves in and out of the body. No need to slow it down or speed it up; just see if it is possible to keep your attention on your own breath for a while. If you find your mind wanders, just take note of this fact and return to focus on your breathing. And that's it. Try this now and then read on after a few minutes.

So – what happened? All sorts of things are possible depending on who you are and what state of mind you were in at the time. You may have become aware of aspects of your breathing that you hadn't noticed before, or you may have found that within seconds your mind was off wandering along in its own sweet way following its own sweet path. Either, or anything else for that matter, is probably normal. All you have noted is what happens when you make it your intention to bring your attention to a certain point of focus. This is the basic principle behind a number of 'focus' practices that take up the first part of the course.

Once there is the tiniest degree of focus developing, however, we begin to move into practices that more directly encourage *awareness* of what is going on in our own experience. We tend always to begin with some form of practice that enables focus, and then move into beginning to take more note of the experiences we are having in our bodies, in our feelings and in our thinking; once again, this is always in a non-judgemental way. We encourage one another not to decide whether a particular experience is good or bad but just to notice it as an experience.

We even try to see thoughts in the same light. I may be harbouring angry thoughts towards my neighbour or critical thoughts about my friend, but at this stage we are simply learning to see these as thoughts that are present in our experience. 'How interesting!' I might be heard to say one too many times in the teaching sessions. But actually this is the point – to bring curiosity and wonder to what we are experiencing, not judgement.

The awareness practice

This can be more difficult to experience at first, but you could try extending the focus practice above by staying just that bit longer with the focus of your attention on the breath. When (not if!) you notice that your mind has wandered, simply take note of what it has wandered to, then come back to your focus on the breath. Spend as long as you choose doing this, as the same thing will probably happen over and over again. Try it now before reading on.

What happened this time? What did you notice? Whatever you noticed, this is awareness. It can seem very simple to start with but equally can reveal the most profound things to us. Of particular interest can be noticing our minds acting in the same way or being drawn to the same subject over and over again. There is still no need to judge or analyse what is going on – just being aware of it is of enormous value.

The third type of practice, which we teach in the *Frantic World* course (but which, for particular reasons, is not incorporated in some other courses), is compassion or 'kindness'. Now this is an interesting thing to include in an apparently 'secular' course. How can kindness be a 'practice'? How can one learn compassion? Isn't it just something you feel or you don't feel? Well, as it happens, it is not really about feelings at all, but about developing an attitude of kindness both to ourselves and to others. The good news for those of us who don't find that this necessarily comes naturally is that it *can* be practised and learned. I will look into this practice and its implications for Christians in detail in Chapter 13; here I am just noting its existence as part of the course. What it involves is the repeated saying of certain phrases that express kindness and compassion, first towards oneself and then towards selected others in our imagination, including people we may find we feel very little compassion for. For some this is quite a challenging practice but for others it has a great beauty to it. For all of us, though, it is a key part of the course and one that comes to colour all the other practices.

The kindness practice

Again, you could try something very simple here. You can sit exactly where you are, close your eyes, imagine yourself sitting here, and say this phrase: 'May I be kept safe and may I know kindness.' You could say it several times. Try this now and notice how it feels to be saying these words.

What did you notice? It may feel very moving – or it may not! It may even feel awkward and create some sort of reaction in you. Whatever you feel, what you have done is to begin – just begin – to cultivate an attitude of kindness towards yourself. There is a long way to go but it is worth discovering how it feels just to have made a start.

So, these are the three basic types of practice we teach over the eight weeks. Of course, the object is not to enable people to become good at meditation practice but to help us to become more mindful in daily life. This is where the benefits come. We add in a number of other kinds of practice that help to bridge the gap between our formal practice, which we are likely to do at the beginning or the end of the day, and the rest of our lives. We have something we call the 'three-minute breathing space', which can be practised at any time of the day when you might be able to create some sort of brief pause (it doesn't actually have to be precisely three minutes). We also have 'mindful activities', where you might choose to carry out a simple task but in a more mindful way. And we even have 'habit releasers', which can be quite fun. These are designed to help us to notice the ruts we can get stuck in; through changing a very simple, habitual way of doing something, we may find we have opened up to a whole new experience that we might not otherwise ever have encountered.

So, that was a whirlwind tour of one version of the eight-week course, intended to give you just a glimpse of the process. If you would like to experience mindfulness to the full, I strongly advise you to join a course run by a trained teacher, or follow one of the courses mentioned at the back of this book.

I have been teaching the *Frantic World* course in the parish context for four years, with very little adaptation of the material. I made an early decision not to mix in spirituality, so that the basic good of mindfulness could come through as clearly as possible. However, I do start by dedicating the evening to God and then inviting people to trust the God we have invoked to look after them in whatever happens through the evening, and we finish with a blessing. I have found it challenging, fun and enormously fulfilling to teach. The real joy is in receiving the feedback forms and hearing many participants (though never all) describe how mindfulness is making such a difference to their lives. And this is the point: it really does work for a lot of people. But, as one Christian member noted towards the end of the eight weeks: 'Yes, I see very clearly now the emotional and psychological benefits of mindfulness, but what about the spiritual aspect?' At the time I was only able to say that it was for him, and each one of us, to find out for ourselves, as we incorporate what we have learned into our own spirituality. In some ways I still stand by this, but for Christians this does seem to be a question that keeps coming up. The rest of this book attempts to offer some possible responses.

2

Mindfulness in the Christian tradition

Mindfulness in the Christian contemplative tradition

As he would be the first to admit, mindfulness was not invented by Jon Kabat-Zinn! As a Buddhist friend of mine once said in response to someone's lazy assertion that mindfulness had been invented in America 25 years ago: 'Perhaps you should change continents and add on a couple of noughts!'

But many will quite rightly argue that something very similar to mindfulness has been around in the Christian tradition since the beginning too. We haven't called it mindfulness. We've called it 'silent prayer' or 'contemplative prayer', 'the desert tradition' or 'mystical theology', but it has been there from Jesus, through St Paul, all the way up to the present. Kim Nataraja, in her book *Journey to the Heart*,[3] gives a very good account of the development of the Christian contemplative tradition through the centuries. She includes chapters on four people in the twentieth century who 'went East', engaged with the Eastern forms of this tradition and probably come closest to Christian mindfulness: Bede Griffiths, Henri Le Saux (Swami Abhishiktananda), Thomas Merton and John Main. Anthony De Mello and most recently Martin Laird also teach about prayer in a way that is consistent with mindfulness practice. These are all Christians from the Western tradition who have been influenced by Eastern spirituality, suggesting that it is not necessarily Buddhism itself that mindfulness is linking in with but perhaps a more general spirituality coming from the East that can just as well be Christian as Buddhist or Hindu.

So mindfulness is not alien to our tradition and we will find huge overlaps with Christian writers. But I still feel that mindfulness, with its Eastern influences and scientific adaptations, can offer much to Christianity. In fact I would go further to suggest that Christianity (especially the Western forms) urgently needs to take on board the insights of mindfulness, and there are three things in particular I would like to note here.

First, there is the particularly Western emphasis on the intellectual, with the corresponding caution, if not downright mistrust, of our experience. We are rightly proud of our intellectual tradition in the West but there has been an equivalent danger of seeing spirituality as something that happens primarily in the head in terms of pure, beautiful and 'correct' thoughts *about* God. This is part of spirituality, certainly, but our heads won't get us to God, partly because God will always be beyond thoughts, ideas and images and partly because it is an *experience* of God that we need – and our minds represent only a very limited part of our experience. Mindfulness can help to redress this balance as it continually draws our attention to the importance and value of our experience in the whole of our bodies in each present moment.

Second, the Western tradition has a history of negative attitudes towards the body as well as the material in general. We have intrinsically picked up that the body and its desires represent a problem, luring us away from the purity and superiority of the mind. But God made us mind *and* body; furthermore, having made us in this way, God declared us 'good'. The mindfulness tradition cuts across this hierarchical separation between mind and body, giving great respect and non-judging attention to the body, seeing the mind–body as a unity. Indeed, it opens up the possibility that very often it is the body's own 'intelligence' that holds the key to many situations. The emphasis in mindfulness on the use of the breath or the body as our focus, compared to the 'prayer word' or 'prayer phrase' used by some traditions, is an important part of this. In fact, I have even wondered whether mindfulness' focus on the body rather than directly on the divine is what *makes space* for us to encounter God in an experiential rather than an intellectual way. But I will allude to this further as the book develops.

Third, we need to consider the consequences of our over-emphasis, in Western teaching, on personal sin and judgement. I fully accept that there are actions I may take that are harmful both to myself and to others and that these actions often originate in the mind or with body impulses. But many testify nowadays that the way we have spoken about these things and the guilt and shame that has been evoked has not, actu-ally, led to changed lives. In fact it seems more often that it has led to a very harmful kind of repression and a rejection of the aspects of ourselves that have become associated with the shame. Mindfulness, on the other hand, helps us to become aware of ourselves, our thoughts and our body impulses in a non-judgemental way. Greater awareness of these things and their possible consequences will be what leads us to choose better actions, not shame and repression. Even addictions have been shown to have been helped by mindfulness practices.

All these things are forms of the 'dualism' that has marked recent centuries of Christian development in the West. Gradually we are coming to see such leanings as an aberration from earlier forms of faith and certainly not helpful for the path towards wholeness.

The Gospels, though, seem to me to be full of this more holis-tic approach to spirituality. I would like to use the rest of this chapter to explore some key Gospel stories that in my view illustrate something of what mindfulness might be all about.

Mindfulness in the Gospels

The parable: 'waking up'

When he came to his senses, he said: 'How many of my father's hired servants have food to spare, and here I am starving to death!'

(Luke 15.17 NIV)

The parable of the prodigal son is a beautiful story and one that perfectly illustrates the sense of awareness we are trying to explore. Have you ever had the experience of suddenly 'coming to' while being fully awake, in the normal sense of the word, all the time? Maybe you were driving along without really thinking (or without realizing you were thinking) and suddenly you realized you were, in your mind, deep in conversation with, say, the owner of the local corner shop about a new charge for delivering your newspaper. Perhaps the first thing you were aware of was the sound of your own voice crying out, with some feeling: 'But that's ridiculous – we have never been charged before!' And suddenly you realize where you are and what you have been thinking about for the past who knows how long. Well, this is what happened to the prodigal – only in a much more serious way.

He had made some choices and followed them through on a very long journey until he was miles from home. He would have had to think quite carefully, on one level, about travel, board and lodgings, choices of various forms of entertainment to spend his money on, and the various business transactions required along the way. So, his brain was indeed operating, perhaps very effectively. But in another sense he was sleepwalking, with no real awareness of where he was going or where he would inevitably end up. It seems so obvious to the reader – especially the reader who is so familiar with the story. How could he not see what was going on? And yet we are all like this in some respect – only partly aware of what is going on under our very noses, only partly awake to the full truth of our own experience. Often we can look back and wonder what on earth we were up to – why didn't we see? But at the time we simply weren't aware.

In the prodigal's case it was only when he was reduced to absolute poverty that he 'came to his senses', as the NIV and TEV put it. In other words, there came a moment when he 'woke up' from his dream and realized where he was and what he was doing. Only then did he recognize the fact that he did have a choice. He could carry on as he was, or he could return to his father and start again.

We are only ever partly awake – partly aware. If we want to know God and God's will for us, we need to wake up to where we are and what we are doing. But how will this happen? Sometimes it takes a traumatic event to wake us up – often something tragic or painful. But how much better it would be if we spent time practising waking up. This is what mindfulness practice does.

The prodigal son practice

Try setting your mobile phone alarm for some random time in the day. Or better still, get someone else to set it for you so you don't know when it will go off. Then when it does, let that be your moment of awakening. Invite yourself to 'come to your senses' and notice where you are, what you are doing, what thoughts were going through your mind and what mood you are in. Then notice what choices are there before you. You could carry on with what you were doing, but equally you may have other choices. It doesn't matter too much what you choose to do. The important point here is that you have woken up and have discovered you have choices before you.

In the course I teach we set up 'prayer buddies' where people pair up and exchange mobile phone numbers. They are then invited to text a '+' to each other regularly, once a day or three times in the week. I find that the effect is twofold. One is the encouraging thought that someone is thinking about me at that point, and the other is to accept it as an opportunity to wake up, come to my senses, notice what is happening in my own experience and see what choices there are before me.

The vignette: 'being' and 'doing'

There is need of only one thing. Mary has chosen the better part.

(Luke 10.42)

The visit of Jesus to Mary and Martha is an oft-quoted little story, especially by those who would advocate the contemplative life above the active life. Jesus appears to make a very clear judgement between the two sisters – against the one who was doing all the work and in favour of the one who simply sat at his feet and listened. 'But', so many of us might protest, 'I would love to just sit and listen too, but the food won't cook itself!' Or (comedic couch-bound teenager's version), 'The beer isn't just going to leap out of the fridge into my hand while you sit there meditating!'

And this, of course, is a very good point. I remember the time a preacher finally opened this passage up to me by saying that there was a bit of Mary and a bit of Martha in all of us. We are not one or the other, but perhaps we ought to understand this as two ways of being in life. There is work to be done, surely. But if our lives end up simply consisting of one task after another, what value does that have? How can we know what tasks have real value or which of so many tasks is the most important? I don't think we can assume that Jesus is saying that sitting and listening is per se better than getting the work done. But he may have been suggesting that there are two ways of being in life, and that we need both, but Mary's way is of primary importance. Taking time to sit and to become aware of Jesus' words to us must be our starting point. Becoming more fully aware of the big picture must take priority before we rush to do stuff.

The trouble is that for many of us 'doing stuff' is all we know; sitting and listening (even though we may complain that we don't get the chance to do it) is a bit of a closed book. So, once again, this needs practice; and interestingly, through practice we can develop an ability to be aware of the situation and Jesus' words to us, even while we are doing the tasks. Mindfulness, then, helps to develop this kind of awareness.

The Mary and Martha practice

The next time you find yourself doing one of those simple but necessary tasks around the house – let's say the washing up – see if it is possible to do it with greater awareness. First, become aware of the task itself and the detail of the activity you are involved in (the feel of the warm, soapy water on the hands, the patterns on the plates, the shapes the leftover food has made, and so on); and then become aware of yourself and your thoughts, of the wider project that you are contributing to (for example, the harmony of the household), of the perceived justice or injustices involved in your being the one who is doing this, of the others who may benefit, and perhaps even God's words to you at this moment.

Is it possible in this way to inhabit something of both Mary and Martha all at once, but perhaps to give greater emphasis to the Mary side of ourselves than we usually do when engaged in such activity?

The prophet: 'making way'

Prepare the way of the Lord, make his paths straight.

(Mark 1.3)

It could be said that John the Baptist is to Jesus as mindfulness is to prayer or the work of God. John came not to save; not to do the work himself, but to help people get ready so that when the moment arrived – when the Saviour came – they would be in a place where they were ready to receive what Jesus had to offer.

Mindfulness itself does not fix things but seeks to open up a space where things might (if appropriate) be fixed. In fact, it teaches us more about *not* fixing things and about learning that it is not our place to try to save ourselves. But it does teach us the skill of opening things up – bringing concerns to the surface – so that, in God's time and in God's way, they might be healed or restored. Jesus talked about how what is hidden will be disclosed and what is secret will be brought to light (Mark 4.22). This is what mindfulness does. Then, when things are disclosed and in the light, there is the chance that God can be more a part of them so that healing or 'fixing' may come.

John the Baptist exercise

Here is a thought or prayer exercise. Bring to mind something in your life that you think possibly, or probably, needs fixing. Now see if it is possible to play the part of John the Baptist; resist the temptation to actually find solutions to the situation – perhaps even noticing how many solutions your mind keeps coming up with automatically – and then simply look at the situation to see if you can perceive it more clearly, perhaps with a deeper understanding. Reflect on the roles various people have played in the scenario, including your own role. But then choose not to come to any conclusion about it; simply leave the situation in God's hands – just for a while, as long as is possible. Then see what happens. In this way we are getting things ready – preparing the way – but not doing God's work. We are leaving room for the work of grace.

And there's more . . .

When I started sharing these passages with a group of mainly Christians who had just completed a mindfulness course, a number of other passages with a possible connection with mindfulness began to come to mind. Briefly, here are some of them.

- On learning the way of not striving: 'Look at the birds in the air; they neither sow nor reap nor gather into barns, and yet your heavenly Father feeds them. Are you not of more value than they?' (Matthew 6.26).
- On learning to live in the present moment: Jesus proclaimed, 'The time is fulfilled, and the kingdom of God has come near' (Mark 1.15); 'Give us each day our daily bread' (Luke 11.3).
- On learning to perceive in a different way (not primarily intellectual or cognitive): Jesus declares that the purpose of the parables is that 'they may indeed look, but not perceive, and may indeed listen, but not understand' (Mark 4.12).
- On receiving physical sight as a metaphor for waking up and receiving spiritual sight: the discourse in John's Gospel after Jesus healed the blind man (John 9). Amusingly, the Pharisees just don't get it!
- On waking up to something that has been under our noses all along: the disciples who eventually recognized Jesus when he broke the bread at the end of the road to Emmaus (Luke 24.13–31).
- On the primary dynamic of spirituality as 'being' not 'doing': Jesus told us to 'Abide in me as I abide in you' (John 15.4).
- On the wisdom of creating space to become aware rather than just react: Jesus' writing in the dust after being brought the woman caught in adultery (John 8.1–6).

There is a danger, of course, when you have started to think about mindfulness, to read mindfulness into every Scripture text you come across, but there seems to be enough here to give us a certain confidence that, far from straying away from Jesus' spirituality, we appear to be straying right into the heart of it.

3

My journey to mindfulness

For the final chapter in Part 1, I come to my own story. In a sense this is just another way of looking at mindfulness from a different perspective, but it may be of interest in terms of how mindfulness came to be such an important part of one particular Christian's life. So, what about my own beginnings in faith, and how did I, after about 30 years of seeking to live the Christian life, find my way to considering mindfulness as a key door to my spiritual practice and even how it could be a key gift to the Church at large?

'All beginnings are hard.' This is the opening sentence of the novel *In the Beginning* by Chaim Potok.[4] The phrase has always moved me and keeps returning to me. This is partly because of the note of compassion in the voice of the narrator – these words are spoken by a traditional Jewish father to his son, David Lurie, who is finding a new school difficult – and partly because the book itself moved me deeply and expressed and continues to express something of my own searching in faith. David grows up with an increasing desire to explore the roots – the beginnings – of his own Jewish faith and through this to find a way of inhabiting the faith for himself in his rapidly chang-ing world. One reason it comes to mind now, as I seek to lay the foundations of this book on mindfulness, is because, built into the principle of mindfulness, is the intention to 'start where you are' – and in so many ways, this is the hard part! I would so like to be able to begin from somewhere else, either to avoid where I am now or because I simply can't see a way forward in my faith, or in my life, starting from this point. But this is the first bit of good news: all beginnings may be hard, but at least we can all start, because the starting point is wherever and whoever we are.

Coming to be fully aware of and present in where I am is a process that mindfulness practice can help with; this is so important, and it is why I am taking time to lay down something of my own beginnings. This is a personal account of mindfulness and how it might be valuable for Christians. It is also practical, rooted in my own twofold experience of having spent three decades exploring the spiritual life in the Christian tradition, and now having become a qualified teacher of mindfulness. I feel myself to be an expert in neither, but an honest struggler and enquirer in both.

I too have always found beginnings hard – but also exciting and brimming with possibility. I have been on a search all my life for something, although I'm not always sure what. Peace to counter the inner turmoil? Yes. For a sense of security to counter my unease with uncertainty? Yes. For a sense of life in all its fullness? Certainly – and more: for meaning, for purpose, for challenge, for a sense of being alive, yes, all of these things. Every time I read a book or choose a film to watch I am searching once again for the person who experiences life as I do and who might just be able to open up a new world for me. And always I am searching for God, who I perceive to be the source and author of all of the above. Every new experience is a new possibility, the hope of peeling back a layer to find not just one more experience but the heart and root of all experience. There is a magnificent passage in *In the Beginning* where David is taking a walk and finds himself slipping from the path down a steep slope. He scrambles desperately to reach back up to the top but most of his effort seems only to go towards displacing a large amount of earth, exposing all manner of roots, seeds and emerging plants. This is the metaphor for his lifelong search for what is beneath, what lies below, what gives cause to the layer above. This is how his faith gradually becomes increasingly authentic for him, and how he learns to own the faith of his Orthodox father despite struggling to accept the particular way his father has lived it.

It is tempting to read back into my own journey this basic paradigm, which has only become apparent to me over time . . . so I will! It seems to me that where I am now is the result of many, many shifts along the way, all in some sense leading to here: all were stages on the road to what I so deeply value in faith today – a sense of awareness and a sense of being.

It all started in a very ordinary churchgoing family. My parents were 'Church of England' rather than consciously Christian, if you know what I mean. My father, who had spent some years in the Indian army, once told me he was more Hindu than Christian. But clearly, a Church of England kind of Hindu! My earliest memories of this kind of faith were mostly positive. The regularity, the familiarity and the routine gave me a sense of order and of reassurance – that all was well. But by my mid-teens, of course, it had become boring. I was looking for life, for freedom, and I was looking to rebel. I was not looking to uncover any roots at this stage, but rather intending to jettison the whole thing.

That was, until a Christian rock band came to our school and gave me two things: one was an image of Christianity that was no longer conforming or establishment (these were faded east London hippies straight out of the 1960s), and the second was a breakthrough realization that Christian faith was actually about something I was deeply longing for – a sense of being loved. Jesus loved me, I was told, and I could in some way have a personal, even intimate relationship with this person who loved me – loved *me*. Thus the first layer had been uncovered, and it was, just like all the others, an uncovering through a new awareness – a 'waking up' to a truth I didn't even know might be a truth. I had never articulated the question of whether God or Jesus loved me; I was just somewhat lost in my own world, which had not even considered these possibilities. So, awakening number one was not actually sought. It just happened, I was there, and I grasped it with both hands. I had made my first conscious and intentional move in my spiritual search. But, crucially, it was about love and it was about coming alive.

My spiritual practice in the following years was what we call a 'quiet time'. It involves reading a passage from the Bible, reflecting on it and then talking to God about it, often in some systematic way. In my own case, I moved quite quickly from this format to more of a journal-writing approach. I would read the Bible passage and possibly the short commentary in the Bible reading notes, then I would write my own thoughts in my journal. And these could go on for pages. They were an attempt to make sense of the text, but even more I was trying to make sense of my own experience, which seemed to be far away from the ideal I read in the biblical text. I was experiencing all the normal anxieties, insecurities and occasional depressions of an older teenager, and writing about them in the light of biblical texts often gave me some sense of comfort.

But at the same time my practice clearly left me short of answers. The worship and love I felt in the churches I attended at the time were very important to me, but the answers I was being given to the questions I was asking, although they seemed logical, bore less and less relation to my experience as a young adult. I was torn between what I felt I was supposed to be experiencing and what was actually happening in my inner and personal life. I say 'inner and personal life' because I was not one of those who had the courage to act fully on everything I found I wanted to do; nevertheless, I did want to do stuff and I could not find a way of reconciling how I felt with how I perceived I was supposed to feel. I was being given this vision of purity to live up to, but I knew I was not pure and no amount of forgiveness seemed to help.

Finally, I was ready to leave. I was due to move to a new town and was ready to use this as an opportunity not to go to church at all. This was a bit scary and brought about a new inner conflict. Somewhere in me I still felt that God must be about freedom and life, and that if the God I was being presented with was not enabling me to experience these things then perhaps this was not the true God I longed for and searched for – the one I sensed when I first embraced the notion that Jesus loved me.

As things turned out, though, I moved into a flat that was 200 yards from a church, and this was where I would begin a new and crucially important stage of my spiritual journey. I had begun to explore writers from the catholic tradition (both Anglo and Roman), and in this church I found a formal expression of this spirituality. But what was it that was so important to me here? Well, for one, there was a distinct lack of 'purity' around the place. I was surrounded by people in various states of broken and confused lives; it was an inner urban church with a ministry to the homeless, many of whom had alcohol, drug or mental health problems, and often all three. The lived-out message was no longer about inner purity, but simply about learning to be with one another and accept one another as brothers and sisters in our various states of inner and outer mess. Second, the prevailing spirituality was liturgy – and silent prayer. This was new to me. I had read about it but never actually practised it with others.

So, the two key aspects here of my slow move towards mindfulness were: first, and most important, a shift towards practising accepting who I was rather than always lamenting what I was not and, second, the beginnings of learning silent rather than talking or writing forms of prayer.

Over the following years I set out to explore and practise this new form of prayer with the same commitment I had brought to the 'quiet time'. I started going on retreat to a monastery that had links with the church. I built into my life significant times for silent prayer and began reading all the books that were available in this tradition. Particularly, I read about the 'Jesus Prayer' in works by various Eastern Orthodox writers, and about the contemplative or mystical tradition as expounded by the likes of Teresa of Avila and John of the Cross, known as the Spanish mystics.

The Jesus Prayer became the predominant structure for my prayer life. This involves sitting or kneeling and simply saying this short prayer over and over again, perhaps in front of a candle or maybe an icon. The prayer has various forms but one well-known version is: 'Lord Jesus Christ, Son of God, have mercy on me, a sinner.' We would practise this communally in church on Thursday evenings, and every evening when I was on retreat at the monastery. We would use 'prayer ropes' as an aid. These are the equivalent of the Roman Catholic rosary beads, and consist of strands of wool tied into a circle of knots with a plastic bead every 10 or 25 knots. You say the prayer once on each knot and when you arrive at a bead, you might stop for some silence or say the Lord's Prayer.

There is theological content in the Jesus Prayer, and the four parts could be said to describe the very basics of the Christian faith: Christ is my Lord, he is Son of God, I am a sinner and I need to ask for mercy. I think that's about it, isn't it? But actually, what seemed to be most important about saying this prayer was that it was a way of entering into silence, and in the silence was the possibility of encountering God. According to what is known as 'mystical theology', God is beyond words, beyond images, beyond theology, and only when all these cease is there the possibility of direct experience or true 'knowledge' of God. John of the Cross talked about the threefold path of purgation, illumination and union. All three were to be experienced, not just understood. So, the 'knowing' of God was 'union' – an experiential relationship, rather than an understanding of theological ideas about God.

It was this practice that I could say held me together through these early years of finding my way in the adult world. Having not had the most psychologically stable of upbringings, I was left somewhat unsettled in my mind and heart. I needed a place simply to be before God so that I could find an inner stillness. Once a week I would set aside an extended time to pray, perhaps up to an hour, and I still remember the sense of deep stillness that would often come upon me around the fiftieth minute. That, you may say, is quite a long time to wait for perhaps a few moments of stillness. But once experienced I realized it was totally worth the effort. Here the knowledge that I was loved became an experience and, rather wonderfully, I no longer felt that sense of inner impurity. Rather, there was a sense that I was being held by the loving gaze of purity – and that was enough. It became the source from which I sought to live the rest of my daily life.

Twenty-three years later, and various forms of this basic contemplative practice had sustained my life through the tumultuous changes brought about by marriage, child-rearing and ordination. I survived, and at times even thrived, as a curate, then a team vicar, and now as a vicar where I still live, in Oxford. I had found a profound and apparently ever-deepening spiritual practice that held me, sustained me and continually enriched my life. So, why move – why change?

Well, in short, I hit a wall. Various things had shifted along the way, and my daily morning practice based around saying the Jesus Prayer had dried up. The various and constant thoughts that seemed to flood in the moment I tried to move into silent prayer – what Teresa of Avila called 'distractions' – were now overwhelming me to such an extent that I remember consistently ending up in a far worse mood at the end of half an hour's silent prayer than when I started. When I arrived for breakfast with the family – look out! Now, I knew that prayer was not all about feeling good, but this was getting silly. And it was probably just basic good sense that told me to stop bothering – just for the moment. I continued my morning practice but moved back to doing spiritual reading followed by journal writing, which at least left me in a better mood, though I was unsure of where I was spiritually or what had really gone wrong.

Two things were in the background to this experience. One was a significant increase in stress in my work and it would perhaps not seem surprising that this played itself out in my spiritual practice. Thoughts and ideas were streaming through my mind that were very often negative, self-deprecating or simply all part of the ongoing struggle to resolve issues that seemed somewhat intractable. The support and guidance I had found through the years in silent prayer were simply deserting me. Had God deserted me, then? I didn't think so, but I could see that this just wasn't working. And so I stopped.

The other issue, which had never really been resolved for me, was the one relating to sin and judgement; this is at the heart of so much of our Christian talk and is clearly the focus of the Jesus Prayer. Yes, I understood and accepted that I was imperfect, that I acted from self-centred motives, that I was often driven by greed or pride and that I lacked love. And I also understood that I was forgiven for all of this so that I could start each day again and do my best. But in my heart and in my secret thoughts the accusations continued and dragged me down. Especially when I was stressed or something seemed to go wrong in the parish, although I could cope with the idea that I had made a mistake, the voice that suggested I was therefore a bad person was harder to resist. It was subtle and often I was barely conscious of it, but it was there eating away at me, at times almost paralysing me. All this led to some periods of very low mood. I have never been treated clinically for depression but this vulnerability has been with me all my life and, with these ongoing stresses, it was becoming more apparent. These negative thoughts about myself have always been a key part of the process and I have never really had an answer to them. Talk of sin, unfortunately, only made them worse and did not bring the freedom of forgiveness they were supposed to offer.

So, when my sister-in-law, a GP, lent me a book about mindfulness – not because she knew my state at the time, but because it seemed to her to be a good thing and she wondered what I thought – it was a revelation to me. Here was a form of meditation practice that not only sounded uncannily like Teresa of Avila at times, but appeared to have the answers to the key places where I stumbled in my own practice. Even better, it promised to be able to teach this practice in a structured way over eight weeks! It was based in entirely clinical and non-faith contexts, but something here was clearly pulling me. I hardly dared to think that there might be an answer to my struggles. In fact, I had concluded somewhat that there wasn't an answer within the Christian tradition, since part of the problem (sin and judgement) seemed to be at the core of Christian spirituality. But here was something that came at the same thing from a different angle. Mindfulness was not prayer, I realized, but could it be that an insight from science was going to help me forward? I feel myself to be as much a scientist as a theologian in my intellectual leanings, and am very open to the insights of science, but I hadn't expected that they might have a bearing on my prayer life!

There was enough here for me to recognize that this was something I needed to explore, and when I came to make plans for a three-month sabbatical I decided to make mindfulness the central focus. I signed up for an eight-week course, read as much as I could about mindfulness and began practising. And, in short, it worked! It worked so well for me that I subsequently signed up at the Oxford Mindfulness Centre to train to teach the course and for the past four years have been running a version of it in the parish.

But what was it that worked? Well, as I hope to explain in this book, mindfulness has helped me as a Christian in many, many ways. But at that time there were two key things.

First, the 'distractions'. The way Teresa of Avila described them, I only ever felt them to be a bad thing, and so I saw them as an enemy to be resisted because they were preventing me from actually praying. But the trouble is, the more you battle with them, the stronger they get; in the end, as I have described, the distractions won. In mindfulness, though, we tend not to use the word 'distractions', instead describing them as 'thoughts'. This helps us to realize that there is nothing wrong with them and that the skill we are learning is not to get rid of them but simply to take note of their presence, without being caught up or taken over by them – and in this way they gradually seem to subside in their energy and intensity. What is more, specific practices can help us to learn how to do this. I think it was this in particular, in combination with a number of other practices, that helped me to get a better handle on managing stress, and I have never had a day's stress since. (OK, actually that last bit was, in fact, not true, but it has got a lot better; even in stressful times I have more chance of working things through more quickly.)

Second, sin and judgement, which seemed to keep me locked in my own wretchedness. As I have said, I believe there are actions that are harmful to others, and thought patterns that are harmful to ourselves. But it seems to me that feeling bad about them (guilt or shame) never helped anyone to grow; instead they tend to put you into a downward spiral of avoidance and denial. The non-judging approach of mindfulness was revelatory and appeared entirely consistent with talk of grace. Whatever I actually experienced in my life was no longer judged to be either good or bad, but was to be fully experienced for what it was so that it could be laid bare before God. This, in turn, seemed to give me increased choices as to what was best. It has helped me to accept myself more fully as a human being, too, and celebrate rather than constantly lament who I am.

I would, in time, discover many other delights and answers to unanswered questions through mindfulness, but these were the two key things that drew me in from the start. And, of course, in many ways I am still only just beginning the journey – which feels equally important to me.

But is that it? Have I finally arrived at the end point of my spiritual quest? Well, I hope not. And I very much doubt it.

But for now, mindfulness-based practices have created space for God in my life, transformed the way I manage stress and opened me up more completely to the promised 'life in all its fullness'. There may well be more to come, but this will certainly do for now.

Part 2

FROM BELIEVING
TO KNOWING

————◆————

So, having laid out some foundations, we come to how mindfulness might have a bearing on the first of my two burning questions about faith: does it make sense? Or, what kind of sense can I draw from the claims we make or the language we use in Christian faith?

Throughout my career as a priest I have had people coming up to me, somewhat awkwardly, having clearly taken a while to pluck up the courage, and half whisper something like, 'Tim, I'm not sure I really believe what I am supposed to believe.' Then there is a nervous pause while they wait for my response. I am not sure where this nervousness comes from, as we live in an age where most people have found the freedom to decide for themselves what to believe. But perhaps there is still a hangover from previous generations where it was accepted that the Church had the power to condemn people for their beliefs. So, the person waits with baited breath to find out whether they will still be welcome members of the church. And yet up to now I have never been aware that they are surprised when I have responded, with a surreptitious look around to see who might be listening, with a mock hushed whisper of collusion: 'Join the club!'

How can one simply 'believe what we are supposed to believe' anyway? If it wasn't so tragic a period of church history it would seem rather more comical that the medieval heretic should be saved from death (or from a more gruesome kind of death) simply by reciting a set of words that complied with the church's official doctrine. The church authorities must have realized that this no more constituted a change in a person's actual belief than my declaring that the earth is in fact flat in order to comply with the whim of the day.

My own view is that belief is not about reciting a set of words but about knowing something to be true *in our own experience*. What the Church has stated over the centuries in its official doctrines form important statements of collective belief and an account of the development of those beliefs, not a straitjacket into which we must all intellectually wriggle.

So, having had an unusually large number of people approach me with various forms of this 'confession' in my current church, I decided to start a group, which I called the 'Thomas group'. A good variety of people came along; one even felt the need to ring me up beforehand because he wasn't sure whether he was enough of a doubter to qualify! But the one key principle of the group was that it should be a safe place for people to be honest about what they deeply felt to be true in their own experience and feel encouraged to engage in a respectful enquiring way with the primary aspects of Christian belief as expressed down the centuries.

At theological college I was taught about the difference between 'theology from above' and 'theology from below'. 'From above' was based on the assumption that truths were being communicated via revelation from God to humans and it was our job to get ourselves into a place where we could receive this revelation. 'From below', on the other hand, would start with human experience, and from this perspective we would work our way towards truths about God. Depending on one's view of revelation, both may well have their place; the Thomas group was there to give space for the latter approach.

And this is how I want to tackle this section of the book. There is no space here for a full theological treatise, and anyway that would be somewhat beyond my ability. But what I want to offer is how mindfulness has helped me to reflect on my understanding of God, Jesus and the Holy Spirit. This is a natural approach for mindfulness since it is primarily about how awareness of our experience leads to all the other benefits, including, in this case, how it might enrich our faith as we move from simply believing something in our heads to knowing something in our lives.

4

God is one, God is love, God is now

Many things have been said about God down the ages – far too many for me even to think about trying to be comprehensive here. But it would seem to me that those who have attempted to be comprehensive have slanted towards what matters to them in their own experience – even if it is primarily their own intellectual experience. So, of the multitude of things that could be said about God, I have chosen three that have occurred to me as a result of practising mindfulness. They are: God is one, God is love and God is now.

God is one

Alongside the assertion that 'God is three', 'God is one' is perhaps the most foundational statement about God. But what do we mean by this? One Trinity Sunday when my eldest son was still very young, I was musing over my sermon and declared vaguely in his direction: 'Do you know, Peter, God is three! And, without looking up from the drawing he was colouring in, he immediately replied, 'I'm three too!' And he was – then. However, he's now 22 but God is still three, so this can't have been quite what I meant. Nicholas Lash, in his book *Believing Three Ways in One God*,[5] reminds us that when we say 'God is one' we do not mean that God is one year old, nor do mean that there is only one God as opposed to three Gods. Lash states that this is, in fact, not really a numerical statement at all but one to do with unity or undividedness. In other words, there is no division in God – there are no separate aspects set against one another, vying for dominance or competing for space with one another. There is diversity in God (which is where the 'three' comes in), as there is in God's creation, but it is a harmonious, co-dependent, non-hierarchical kind of diversity. And this is what we mean by God being one.

It is through the practice of mindfulness that I have become increasingly aware in my own experience of how we humans are constantly wanting to divide that which has a natural unity in God. And there are three ways (of course) that humans, through either fear or the desire to dominate or exploit, have tended to divide things up.

First, we have divided ourselves from ourselves. God, we read, made us in God's own likeness, which would seem to suggest that although there are diverse elements in us we should not be divided in ourselves as positive and negative elements, or bits we like and don't like, or even 'spiritual' bits and 'material' bits. And yet psychologists will tell us the degree to which we have become divided selves through the process of repressing those parts of ourselves we find uncomfortable or have learned to be ashamed of, and promoting the parts that seem to be more acceptable to ourselves and others. As we divide ourselves, we offend the unity of God who made all of us as a unity. In mindfulness the consistent practice of paying attention to aspects of ourselves with non-judging awareness is what can begin the process of bringing back into a relationship of unity that which has been divided.

I find that this has become gradually true in my own experience as I reconnect with buried aspects of myself, half-forgotten memories and past experiences. All is brought gradually into a relationship of unity as my awareness develops. And the more this happens, the more I come to understand what it is we mean by God being one. One particular aspect of this dividedness is our tendency to see our minds (or our spirits) as in some way separate from our bodies. There was an early heresy called Gnosticism, which promoted the idea that the mind or spirit was superior to the body and that spiritual enlightenment was somehow about denying the material and escaping into a spiritual perfection where the body no longer held the disciple back. There is still a tendency towards this way of thinking in our own day, which again surely deeply offends the unity with which God made us as body-minds. You cannot divide the two and we should not try to. However, we have done so, and perhaps the 'body scan', such a foundational plank of all mindfulness practice, has a major part to play in restoring our rightful, respectful connectedness with our bodies.

Second, we humans have divided ourselves, in our minds, from other human beings. Evolutionary biologists tell us that this is a deeply ingrained instinct born out of times of scarcity of resources. If there is a sense that there will not be enough for everyone to survive, then instinctively we feel pushed towards dividing people into 'us' and 'them' and in this way justifying to ourselves who gets fed and who doesn't. 'Us' could be just me or it could include my family, my tribe, my nation, my race, my gender or even those with the same sexual orientation as me. But however I divide the cake, I am still dividing what is naturally one in God who made one human family.

And once again, awareness is the key here. As I become increasingly aware of my own experience, I also become aware of the common experience of all humanity and that there is, in essence, no basis for dividing us at all. The mindfulness weekly drop-in session that I run can now claim to be a multi-faith spiritual context with atheists, Jews, Christians and one who 'leans towards Buddhism' attending and sharing in the same practices. The reason we all find we can be together in this is that we are not focusing on the differences between our belief systems but on our common experience in practising mindfulness. We *all* find our minds wandering when we sit down to meditate, whether Buddhist, Christian or Jew (and what a relief it is to discover that we are not the only ones!). Here we find our common humanity, which speaks (to those of us who are theists) of the unity of God. Paying proper, non-judging attention to another's experience will gradually build up the sense of unity I share with the whole human family. And as this sense of unity grows I will be more inclined, in times of scarcity of resources, to find ways of sharing, so that we all survive rather than jumping to the age-old practice of 'divide and conquer'.

Third, we have divided ourselves from the rest of nature. I will return to this subject in Chapter 14, so it is enough to say here that we have applied the same kind of divisive attention to our relationship with nature as we have to both ourselves and other humans. Here is the same 'us' and 'not us' kind of attention, with anything that is 'not us' being considered inferior and therefore able to be exploited for our own ends. 'Us' is now all of humanity and 'not us' is the rest of nature. And yet God is one and all of nature is one, in a perfectly balanced ecosystem that is deeply damaged if one part decides that it is not part of the unity. Chapter 14 describes mindfulness practices that help to reconnect us humans in a proper way to that from which we have divided ourselves in nature.

Our experience of the unity of all things in God may sometimes feel like a distant dream, but we have wonderful encouragements from the glimpses described in our own contemplative tradition: from Teresa of Avila's experience of ecstasy, which she called 'divine union', to Thomas Merton's experience of unity with all human beings, which came to him in a busy high street on his emergence from a long period of solitude. These momentary experiences are not given to us as the norm but as a glimpse of where we are heading and of the unity in God that is the true nature of all things.

So God is one, and everything that there is is one in God. This is not just a neat doctrinal statement but a fundamental description of the whole of reality. Humans have divided up that which is one in God over and over again in order to serve our own greed. Mindfulness is entirely concerned with reconnecting what has been divided and so bringing the unity of God to bear on human experience.

God is love

Here is another one that trots off the tongue very easily, but it deserves the scrutiny of the 1980s pop song, 'What is this thing called love?' What, indeed, is love? Or, more precisely, what do we mean when we say that God is love? I have preached many a wedding sermon in which I have tried to reflect what might be meant by divine love as opposed to the many kinds of human loves. I am vicar of the church that C. S. Lewis attended for 30 years and so a natural source is his book *The Four Loves*.[6] He refers to four different Greek words for love; three of them describe human experiences of love, which he interprets as affection, friendship and erotic love, and the fourth describes divine love which, he says, has a different quality to it altogether. Not being dependent on human whim and fancy, this type of love needs to infuse all the human loves we experience. I find this, on the whole, very valuable. But I also find that I am still searching, not just for an idea but a way of talking about God's love that I can actually experience. Since practising mindfulness I have come to sense a whole new way of describing what might be termed divine love.

As I have suggested, one description of mindfulness is that it is the practice of the art of non-judgemental awareness. The early stages of practising mindfulness can be quite discouraging, since all we experience is (1) our *lack* of awareness and (2) the presence of judgement! And yet just to start noticing that this is what we are like is huge progress in itself. We lack awareness because we have become identified with our own experience – we think we are what we experience because we have not yet found a place to stand from which we can see that our experience is, in fact, transient and no more defines who we are than a riverbank is defined by the water that flows alongside it. The riverbank has been shaped by the water but it is not the water. The water has flowed past and is gone already. If we are in a boat on the river with no rudder and no sail, we are simply carried along and have no perspective on the water that is flowing. It all looks the same because we are caught up in it and are flowing at the same speed. If, on the other hand, we get out of the boat and swim to the bank, we can begin to *see* the water flow by.

So, mindfulness helps us to get out of the boat and on to the riverbank and begin to get some perspective on our own experience. We start to see it happening while we are experiencing it and gain some initial perspective on it. We cannot intentionally love what we cannot see, so taking steps towards greater awareness is the first stage of moving towards where God is – which, I want to suggest, is the place of pure and total awareness. Our tradition has called this 'omniscience' but this has been reduced, it seems to me, to simply the idea of knowing all the information there is to be known, like the contents of my wife's handbag or what is going through the mind of our Labradoodle when she lies on the sofa and stares at me. But awareness feels much more profound than this. It is not just a head full of facts but experiential knowledge: knowledge from the inside, the very inside of another's experience, first-hand knowledge. This is the kind of knowledge God has of us as God gazes upon us with this kind of gentle, loving attention.

So here we have an image of the divine gaze, forever holding us in awareness. In some ways this, in itself, gives meaning to my life – that whatever I am doing and however well or badly my life is going, someone (God, no less!) knows I am here and is aware of my every move and every thought; someone who is not being carried away by my experience as I am, often losing perspective completely, but someone who is in a position to be able to watch my experience as it flows past, seeing it all in the perspective of eternity. Even if I lose perspective, I know it exists, because God is in that place where perspective can be seen. When I am aware of being held in this sort of gaze I feel totally loved – nearly!

I say nearly, because one more element is needed to paint the picture of perfect, divine love, and that is this element of non-judging. This is because we are so conscious of the human propensity for misusing our awareness of others. The moment we humans have knowledge, or the awareness I have described above, we immediately find that we want to use it for our own ends. And in order to make use of my knowledge, I need to judge each aspect as good or bad (or, to be more honest, 'useful for my purposes' or 'not useful'; 'bolstering up my own ideas' or 'challenging to me'). And so we label everything we see in the other as good or bad – something we want more of or something we want to get rid of. The thought of any being holding me in awareness only feels like love if I can trust that this kind of judging is completely absent – and not absent just because the being concerned is working really hard not to succumb to the temptation to judge, but because I know that it is simply not in this being's nature to judge.

So now I have an image of the divine not only holding me for ever in perfect awareness but also forever gazing on every aspect of me without judging me, valuing every part as a part of the whole person whom God created. This is crucial if I am to allow God's gaze to bring me to that unity and wholeness described in the previous section. If I feel judged I will, like Adam and Eve, start to hide parts of myself from God. If I feel loved entirely without judgement, I will gradually dare to allow every aspect of myself to come into the light of God's gaze and so into relationship with the rest of myself – and *this* is how healing comes. Don't forget, in Genesis 1 God declared that it was 'good' – all of it!

You may rightly argue that a lot of judging goes on in the Old Testament in particular, and to some extent in the New. But this is almost entirely judging of particular actions and not of whole people. Yes, wisdom requires us to understand which of our actions cause harm to ourselves, to others or to the rest of nature. But this is nothing to do with the kind of human prejudicial judging that is completely absent in the divine gaze.

This is how I have come to perceive myself to be loved by God. And this is the kind of love I aspire to offer to others: paying attention in such a way that I don't just hear information but begin to perceive the actual experience of the one I am paying attention to, then learning to suspend my natural instinct to judge according to my own values, simply holding what I have become aware of in reverential awe and respect. This is the greatest gift we can offer one another, and it seems to me that the practice of mindfulness has a part to play in helping us to offer it.

God is now!

So, why the exclamation mark? I am clearly in danger of moving us towards the worst kind of election sloganeering. But it just seems to me that this is the one that is the icing on the cake; it brings something of a tingle to my spine, so I thought perhaps an exclamation mark might communicate this(!). 'God is one' and 'God is love' are all very well, but unless 'God is now!' then it all remains a slightly distant theory. 'God is now!' brings it all home, right into the heart of my own experience – which, as I note at other points in this book, is only ever now! (Last one . . . promise.)

Our tradition has another 'omni' word. It is 'omnipresence'. I used to find this a bit unsettling when it was explained to me that it meant that God was everywhere – only, I suppose, because as a small boy I still thought that I could hide things from God. But what if omnipresence was more about time than place? What if God's omnipresence is about God being always (and only ever) in the present moment – only ever in the now? Now that sounds more exciting to me and is exactly what mindfulness practice is consistently trying to point us towards:

there is only now in our experience and so, Christians would add, we can only ever experience God now – in the present moment.

In contrast, here is another way humans feel drawn to dividing up that which has a natural unity. We see time as past, present and future, and instead of being able to rest in the eternal now we live much of our time dominated by the controlling power of the past or anxiety about the future. Thoughts of past or future push us right back into this instinct to push away what we don't like (unpleasant memories of the past, or avoiding thinking about what we feel might be an unpleasant future), or clinging to what we do like (the 'glory days', or an overexcitement about the evening to come), so much so and so often that we persistently miss the simplicity and beauty of the present moment – which is all there is – and, remember, the only place where God is.

Don Cupitt, in his book *Theology's Strange Return*,[7] talks about this as 'eternity breaking into the present moment'. Eternity is not the eternal past or the eternal future but the whole of time, the whole of existence – all that there is, being here in the present moment. Worth turning up for then – or 'waking up' for!

Sam Wells, vicar of St Martin-in-the-Fields, Trafalgar Square, has talked about baptism being the sacrament of the present moment because it liberates us both from the controlling power of the past and from anxiety about the future in order to live freely and gloriously in the present moment – which (do I need remind you?) is where God is!

Many of the 'mystical' experiences of unity referred to in the first part of this chapter also seem to have an element of timelessness in them. Sheldon Vanauken describes, in his book *A Severe Mercy*,[8] being on a yacht with his wife, and out on deck one night there was a moment when somehow the beauty and atmosphere of the moment completely overwhelmed him; afterwards he realized that he had *absolutely no idea of how long he had been standing there*. He had been totally caught up in the timelessness of the moment – unaware of past, present or future – and this was as close to knowing the presence of God as he had ever felt.

Cupitt says this: 'I am suggesting that we can and do regain eternity when we are so immersed in life, in moral action, or in aesthetic contemplation, that we completely forget about time and anxiety.'[9]

What a wonderful way to live, then – so unconcerned with what may have happened in the past and unafraid of what may happen in the future that we are entirely caught up only in the now, and able to experience the present moment for its own sake. This, as I describe further in Chapter 7, is knowing God's presence, and mindfulness definitely has a part to play in helping us to experience this.

5

Jesus: the embodied one, the liberated one, the awakened one

--------◆●◆●◆--------

'Here is the man!' Pilate's words in John's Gospel (John 19.5) as he presents the humiliated Christ to the jeering people contain, for us who have come to revere Jesus, such irony. Pilate's throwaway remark comes across as entirely utilitarian: 'Here you are – I think this is the one you want.' And yet this image of Christ, especially through the many ways it has been depicted in art, and incorporated as one of the 14 traditional Stations of the Cross, says so much more to us. This is *the* man. This is humanity – in perfection. This is what it is to be fully human. Though this is how those who are less than human will treat you for the offence you cause by your humanity.

You don't need to have been practising mindfulness for very long before you start thinking thoughts like, 'Wow, Jesus was a very mindful person. I wonder where he did his eight-week course.' Many of the things we are steering towards in mindfulness are already present in the way Jesus is and how he relates to others: his stillness and dignity in the face of humiliation and suffering; his lack of defensiveness in response to aggressive questioning; his full attentiveness to the people who come to him for help, even in the midst of the hustle and bustle of a demanding crowd; his alertness to the subtlety of the devil's temptations; and yet his honesty and awareness of his own fear in Gethsemane and his experience of abandonment on the cross.

But what is at the heart of all this? What is it about Jesus as *the* man – *the* human being, the one we look to as the model for all of humanity, who might link with our overall theme of the place mindfulness has in Christian faith? We normally try to relate the essence of who Jesus is by referring to the three great moments in his existence on earth: his birth, his death and his resurrection. Let us explore each of these in this context.

Behold, the embodied one

The birth of Jesus is referred to in theological-speak as the 'incarnation': meaning literally the 'in-the-flesh-ness' of God. God, the incarnation reveals, is not actually 'up there' after all, wherever 'there' might be, but is 'down here' in the material world – actually in the flesh and blood of humanity, and most fully and uniquely in the particular human Jesus Christ, '*the* man'. Now, as with many of our familiar theological themes, this may well have lost its full radical meaning for us. Much popular thought drifts towards the comforting notion that God knows what it is like to be a human, with all its struggles and temptations. And that is indeed comforting and encouraging. But it is when we turn this thought round that it begins to offer its full radical meaning. So, what incarnation means for us is that we humans can actually know and experience God in the flesh – in our material bodies and through the material world. In fact, we need to go further and say that our own flesh and blood is the *only* place we can or will *ever* experience and know God. This is really very important, as there is no other place any human can be other than in our bodies (which, of course, includes our brains, the seat of the mind). We have no way of experiencing anything at all, let alone God, other than in our bodies. Our bodies are, in fact, 'it'; if we can't know God in our bodies then we can't know God. The story of Jesus adds to this by suggesting that human beings can (though perhaps only one ever has) have a total experience of God in their bodies. This is perhaps the more radical meaning of the incarnation.

Our bodies, though, can so often be uncomfortable places to be. Our bodies are also the place where we experience suffering, temptation, fear, loss of control. And it may well be that these experiences have led us towards a secret inner longing to be 'free' of our bodies, so that we can live in some blissful, purely spiritual existence. Attractive and even beautiful a thought as this may be, Christianity has always regarded this approach as a heresy. Another tendency, especially some would say in our Western culture, is to subjugate the body by first relegating it to a lower status compared with the mind and then repressing its instincts and drives. But, of course, as we have observed far too often both in our own lives and in spiritual leaders who advocate this approach – it doesn't work! Sex and sexuality is the most obvious example here, and I am forever grateful to Benedict Ramsden, an English priest in the Russian Orthodox Church, who came up with the wonderful line: 'The trouble with you in the West is that you have sex on the brain – which is actually not a very good place to have it!' We have become hung up about sex in the West because we think it is something to think about and 'tame' in some way. But actually sex is to be experienced in the body – and we have plenty of literature, from Song of Songs to Teresa of Avila, that links sexuality with spirituality.

So, neither escaping from our bodies nor repressing them is either effective or Christian. But fully living in and experiencing our bodies as the place where God dwells is what incarnation is about. 'Do you not know', asks St Paul, in 1 Corinthians 6.19, 'that your body is a temple of the Holy Spirit . . .?'

In mindfulness it has been the positive attitude towards the body, and the emphasis on working with the body, that has really brought all this home to me. No longer is the body to be seen as something that is frustrating my spiritual progress; it is to be celebrated and honoured as *the* place where I meet with God! I was exploring these ideas in a talk about mindfulness, and just after we had practised a 'body scan' a woman came up to me and said, 'I am with you all the way with this but it was just that when you asked us to pay attention to our knees I couldn't help thinking, "What has God got to do with my *knees*?!"' I have to sympathize with her. Mine are both knobbly and wonky and would be almost the last thing I would think about if I was contemplating spirituality and the body. However, the obvious answer to this is, 'If God has nothing to do with your knees, then God is not God at all but a lesser being who is "god" of everything in all of creation except your knees!'

Any eight-week mindfulness course will spend at least the first three weeks introducing meditations focused on the body. This can be unpleasant, or extremely boring. For me it was a mixture of the two. I have a stiff and creaky body, and even simple movements and stretches can create very negative feelings in me. But also, for most of my life I have lived in my head, assuming that this is where my salvation lies – where I will work out all my problems and where I will experience God. So I would say I was very disconnected with my body: if not experiencing the annoyance of mild stiffness and pain, I would experience nothing at all – which was very boring. However, I am slowly coming to reconnect with my body, to delight in it and wonder at the glorious fact that it is in this body and in this body alone that I will come to know God.

Jesus is the embodied one – the one who knew and experienced God, fully and completely, in his human flesh and blood. This is the first key to who he is as the paradigm for all humanity.

Behold, the liberated one

There are many ways of thinking about the cross and its meaning for our lives. I want to reflect on it as the event that defined someone who was truly and totally free. But what do we mean by freedom in this sense? In the film *The Lion King*,[10] Simba, the child-prince lion, muses on what it will be like when he is king, thinking of everything he will be able to do that he is not allowed to do now. His father, the king, declares with a sigh: 'Oh Simba, there is more to being king than just doing what you like.' To which Simba replies, without taking a breath: 'There's more?!'

Freedom is perhaps not just about doing what you like, but about being free to be who we are called to be. Jesus clearly had a very deep sense of calling early on in his ministry, which was depicted in his experience at his baptism and in his temptations in the desert. In John's account of Jesus washing the disciples' feet, Jesus is said to have known 'that he had come from God and was going to God' (John 13.3). Yet any number of things might have deflected him from the path that he knew was true for him. He experienced the painful misunderstandings of his own family members and felt he had to step outside the comfort of their protection. His itinerant lifestyle took him away from the security of a stable home environment. He had a developing reputation as a skilful orator and healer, and there may have been a sense of sadness in not being able to develop this, or in jeopardizing this, as he got into confrontation with the authorities. In Gethsemane he clearly sensed what looked like unbearable suffering ahead. And finally, we must assume that he knew that the very likely outcome for someone seen as a troublemaker would be death – especially if he failed to massage the egos of those who would decide his fate. But it was the mark of a man who was utterly and completely free that none of these things persuaded him to abandon who he was and the path that was for him the path of truth and love. Going back to the image of 'Behold, the man', this ragged, beaten, spat-upon human being is for us, ironically, our quintessential image of freedom.

In mindfulness, it is in awareness that we find freedom. The things that control us – take away our freedom – are those that are hidden to us. Gradually, through the ongoing process of bringing awareness to all that is going on within me I have become aware of the hidden fears, insecurities, resentments and controlling compulsions that cause me to be less than free. In the language of St Paul, 'I do not do what I want, but I do the very thing I hate . . . I do not do the good I want, but the evil I do not want is what I do. Now if I do what I do not want, it is no longer I that do it, but sin that dwells in me' (Romans 7.15, 19–20). These are the words of someone describing the time when he was not free – when he was being controlled by as yet hidden compulsions. Jesus had no hidden compulsions or hidden fears. He had fears, but they were not hidden. And because they were not hidden, he was able to experience them rather than be controlled by them, and to choose the way of freedom once again. As I explore further in Chapter 8, this freedom was expressed most fully in his death on the cross – he was not even controlled by what would have been an entirely natural fear of and aversion to death itself. In this way he demon-strated his complete freedom as a human being.

So for us, Jesus is also the liberated one, in whom there was no hidden controlling power to conflict with his freedom. And this is the second key to his being *the* man for all humanity.

Behold, the awakened one

In one of the Anglican eucharistic prayers comes the phrase: '[He] revealed the resurrection by rising to new life' (*Common Worship* prayer B, p. 188). When I link Jesus' resurrection with the idea that he was fully awake, I don't mean that he became awake only after his resurrection, but that the resurrection was what revealed that he was a fully awakened being – and had been all along.

I realize that we are more familiar with the phrase 'awakened one' from Buddhist teaching than in Christianity, and in par-ticular it describes the Buddha himself. But actually many in the Buddhist tradition would not claim the phrase exclusively for followers of the Buddha; they are happy for it to be used to describe anyone who has become fully awake, by whatever path.

So what does it mean to be fully awake? Well, first, as I was suggesting in the previous section, there would no longer be any hidden controlling factors in our lives. Everything that might affect, control or influence the choices we make has come to the surface and we are now 'awake' to them. But I wonder whether being fully awake also means that we have woken up to the extraordinary scope of human potential in life. It is hard for me to speak of this, as one who is very much not fully awake, and generally prefers to stay half asleep with my limited choices (and crucially, therefore, my limited responsibility!), but the extraordinary nature of the resurrection narratives cannot but nudge me towards the possibility that there is more to human experience than I have yet woken up to. Whether it means that I may one day be able to walk through walls, heal people of diseases (or bad knees) or walk on water, I don't know, but I sense in my bones that there is more. And if there is more, then it comes as a calling to explore it and to live it – for God's sake.

Right at the beginning of the *Matrix* trilogy,[11] the futuristic science fiction films by the Wachowskis that depict life after computers have finally(!) taken control of the planet, most humans are having a very pleasant, benign experience of life, being fed, directly into their brains, a series of restful images by the computers that are now ruling the world in anything but a benign way. The reality is that all these humans are in fact being preserved in vats of 'goo' so that the heat from their bodies can be used as energy to drive the computers. Their benign experiences are, indeed, only in their minds. Every now and then there comes a human who, despite being fed with the same peaceful images, senses that there must be something more, and whose mind starts exploring such possibilities. There then comes a point when these individuals, in their mind-experience, are offered a choice of two pills: one that will send them back to their comfortable and pleasant non-awakened life or one that will wake them up to full reality. Choosing the reality pill bucks the computer system and they are ejected from their vats of 'goo' and start living a harsh, but at least real, 'awakened' life. The Christ-type figure in this story is known as Neo – so called, we later discover, as it is an anagram of One. This is 'the One' who, in his fully awakened state, is then able to undermine the power base of the computers and release all of humanity from their half-lives of comfortable but meaningless sleep. What a wonderfully well-worked analogy of the state we humans are in – only half awake, yet increasingly kept comfortable and at ease by the technology we thought would liberate us.

The resurrected Christ reveals to us what fullness of human living might be for someone who has finally and fully woken up to all that there is. While we are not fully awake to all of reality, we are living a half-life. So, waking up and becoming fully aware is the path to fullness of life, and this waking up is at the very heart of what mindfulness practice is all about.

Jesus is, then, the fully awakened one who beckons us to follow him – to dare to wake up to all of life.

6

The Holy Spirit: free will, decentring

In the last two chapters we reflected on aspects of the nature of God and the essence of who Jesus is for us. So, what else is left? Well, there is us, of course – mere human beings. What does it all mean for us and how can any of this become a reality? I like to think that this might have been roughly the conversation taking place between the disciples on the day of Pentecost. 'Well, that was all pretty wonderful – but now what?!' They had managed to choose a successor to Judas but that was pretty much it. Then something rather extraordinary happened – so extraordinary that no one could quite describe the experience, although there was talk of flames of fire spreading round the room and the sound of a 'violent wind' (Acts 2.1–4). And from then on they never looked back. The last part of the jigsaw had fallen into place, and all that was true of Jesus was now being made available to the disciples – although judging by their very human adventures from here on, they were only actually able to receive what was being offered bit by bit.

So the Holy Spirit, it seems to me, is all about how all this can become real for us in our own lives – how we too can live the embodied, liberated and awakened life that Jesus showed was possible for human beings.

Christians have called this the process of 'sanctification', and because it naturally involves every aspect of the human being, many books have been written about its various and diverse elements. I would like to choose two aspects (yes, just the two this time!), which relate to how mindfulness might be making space for the Holy Spirit to work within us.

Free will

First is the thorny matter of free will, which our idea of human sanctification is entirely based upon. God does not force us to become holy people. At every stage it must be our own choice to engage in this process. But is there such a thing as free will? Both philosophers and scientists (particularly some neuroscientists) have called it into question. The arguments are actually quite nuanced,[12] but here are the broad ideas.

Philosophers have argued that it is quite possible to imagine that every decision we take is pre-programmed at the moment of our conception by the particular set of genes we inherit. Everything we do is something we would do anyway, wouldn't we, because of our genes. Neuroscientists since the early 1980s (following Benjamin Libet of the University of California) have added to this with brain experiments that seem to imply that in many cases we 'decide' to do something fractionally before we become aware of the *sense* of deciding to do it. The argument runs that most, if not all, of our choices are made by our unconscious minds without reference to our conscious minds (with which we would normally associate our free will); therefore, no free will. The perception of free will is merely the experiential realization that we have already decided!

As I have said, I regard myself as a scientist as much as a theologian, so I want to take this research very seriously. But, perhaps surprisingly, I think it helps us in our quest. The conclusion I would draw from these experiments is that 'choices' are in fact being made but it is just that more than we realize are made by our unconscious minds; our conscious minds only become aware after the 'choice' has been made. In other words, our choices may be made automatically and compulsively, based on previous conditioning rather than necessarily on the full awareness of what is going on in the present moment. I still want to call these 'choices' but it is just that we are unaware, or not fully aware, of them. This gives a very narrow way in, but a way in nevertheless. I may have to accept that my free will is limited, but even the smallest amount of free will can be used to choose to bring my awareness towards the place where 'choices' are being made, and start from there. A bit like Jesus' mustard seed of faith, you need only the very tiniest amount for it to grow into something so huge that it can help you to move mountains. Use whatever free will you have, then, and it can gradually grow into a mountain for you.

The work of mindfulness is to help us to move towards that place where choices are being made, even if they are unconscious, and to begin to make those choices conscious ones (or free ones, as far as our conscious minds are concerned), which is what I would define as 'free will'. The trouble is that as we begin to practise this we may well become rather frustratingly aware of all the things in which we seem to have no free will: I can't control my thoughts; I can't stop judging myself; I can't relax just when I want to; I can't stop worrying about this or that; I can't forgive. This is why the advice is just to watch it all happening; there is so much we want to change but will simply not be able to, and we will only create stress by trying. So, just watch it all and start by accepting, as neuroscience suggests, that we do in fact have very little free will. But what is actually happening as we do this is that we gradually allow what is usually unconscious to become apparent to the conscious mind. We begin to get more and more of a look-in at how the unconscious mind works and the process by which it is making its decisions; then, as the decision-making process is slowly exposed, our conscious minds might eventually be able to have a say in what goes on. Jonathan Haidt, in his book *The Happiness Hypothesis*,[13] describes this as being like a rider trying to steer an elephant. The momentum is always with the elephant but as long as there is a rider at all then she or he can gradually develop the skills for how to affect the will even of the elephant. And the rider, of course, has to develop some quite subtle skills that have little relation to the comparative physical strengths of the two mammals.

A good illustration here is from the world of addiction. Most addicts have long since given up on the notion that they might have any choice in their addiction. Their experience, and belief, is that they have no choice – they cannot do anything else but have another cigarette or another drink. They believe this partly because they are (almost completely) right and partly because the moment they are aware of the idea of choice, it is too late. The decision has already been made: they are already halfway to the shops to buy their next pack of 20 or the full-blown idea of a drink and its consolations is formed in their minds and there is only the sense of helplessness in the face of the apparently inevitable. If, however, they have been working away at developing their sense of awareness such that they are able to notice the very first stirrings that they know will lead to the next drink *before* the actual decision is made within them – for instance, when they first sense that slight disappointment in themselves or hear the voice that puts them down or feel that sense of failure or hurt – and to notice the moment when real choice is still open to them, then perhaps, just perhaps, different choices could be made that might avoid ever coming to that place of inevitability. The condemning voice, for example, might be recognized for what it is – just a voice – and there may be a realization that several choices are available at this stage, of which having a consoling drink is only one. It may take a while before they are able to choose something different, but it all starts with recognizing the moment at which we still have choice.

This is a long, slow path for an addict, and not nearly as simple as it may sound here. I was very moved by the story of a member of one class I helped to teach who was a recovering alcoholic. Around the sixth week of the course his mother died. This was not a shock, but nevertheless it was a highly emotional experience for him. Such an event, he related to us in the session after she had died, would in the past have been the sure beginning of the slippery slope towards his next drink. But because he was on the course and practising mindfulness regularly, he found he was able to notice the initial familiar feelings right at their outset; he remembered that he had a choice and decided to do something different (in his case, a very short mindfulness practice) to support himself. He found that he was able to respond differently.

One more anecdote from the world of science is intriguing here. Another study, which was neutral as regards the existence of free will, was used to assess the difference in *behaviour* between people who believed in free will and those who didn't. Those who believed in free will turned out to be significantly more altruistic than those who didn't. So perhaps it is true that believing in free will is what motivates us to find the place where it actually exists and then build on it.

A woman who suffered from depression provided one of the most moving and authentic bits of feedback I have received on any course. In response to being asked for one thing that she had learned during the course, she said simply, 'I have discovered I have more choices.' Finding the place where we still have a choice, I would suggest, is how we can let the Holy Spirit affect our lives.

Decentring

Another barrier to the Holy Spirit's work is, well . . . me. They tell me it is not all about me but it clearly is. I haven't quite worked out how it can also be all about you (as you may well suggest, and that seems a reasonable proposition), but still it clearly is all about me. I see everything in the world through *my* eyes and from *my* perspective and I experience it in *my* head – and yes, mostly in my head, as I am still only a beginner in the body thing.

So my own, primarily head-centred perspective is everything. The only trouble is that life just doesn't appear to work very well with this fundamental thought as its basis. Rather more shocking is that the Holy Spirit does not seem to be solely concerned with me but just as much with the whole of creation; in fact, not necessarily with me always as the centrepiece or even me as the starting point! My 'me' perspective is actually rather a large barrier not only to the Holy Spirit sorting me out but to my enabling the Holy Spirit to work through me at all. Oh dear! In order to allow the Holy Spirit to work in me and through me, a process of decentring needs to happen so that I can begin to move towards the place and basis upon which the Spirit works at all – that is, for the good of all of creation.

A little potted history of five centuries of Western intellectual thought may help us here, each of three phases being set off by a new scientific discovery – or, in the language of this book, a new stage of human awareness.[14]

Around 500 years ago, Copernicus, followed by Galileo, offered the truly shocking proposition that the earth was not the centre of the universe but rather that we were a small planet revolving around our sun, which was one among many. Subsequently, we have discovered just how not-the-centre-of-the-universe we really are: a tiny insignificant planet, hardly a spec in what may be one of thousands of universes. The Church – or was it really 'the establishment', in which the Church was central? – reacted negatively not because they could argue with the science but because the shift in conscious perspective was just too massive. Our view of ourselves as humans was that God had chosen us as the centre of everything, so our planet must surely also be at the centre. This discovery was impossible to grasp at the time, and led to the futile business of recantations being demanded or heads would roll.

However, gradually the establishment opened up to this new idea. All was more or less accepted until, 400 years later, Darwin set off the next wave of decentring of human consciousness. The implications of his thought, which again I would suggest was the real difficulty people had with his work, was that humans were not even the centre of the natural world. We are just one among many living beings – and in fact no more, in essence, than a particularly advanced ape. We are unique, perhaps, in that we possess a very developed consciousness and self-awareness and so bear a particular responsibility for the care of the world, but we are not the centre – not the ones around whom every-thing else revolves. Ever so slowly, we have begun to see our-selves, then, as a part of a delicately balanced ecosystem, which will be damaged beyond repair if one of the parts starts to dominate at the expense of every other part. This second decen-tring of human consciousness was, however, as hotly contested as the first.

The third wave of the decentring of human consciousness has come with the modern study of medicine and especially the emergence in the 1990s of something called 'neurogastroen-terology'(!!).[15] This area of study increasingly suggests that the brain is not even the centre of the human being, but rather that our neurological awareness or intelligence is shared with the whole body. This has been expressed in our language in the past but we have tended to assume that it was merely metaphor: we have a 'gut feel' for something, we need to 'get something off our chest', we know something 'in our hearts' and so on. But now we are coming to understand that there is scientific truth in these sayings. The body sends important, 'intelligent' messages to the brain just as much as vice versa, and what's more, the body is often right where the brain has got itself in a muddle.

Wisdom, then (often noted as the Old Testament precursor to the Spirit), is what comes with this decentring of human consciousness. God cares for us and perhaps wants us to have a unique role, but we should not see ourselves as the centre. Not everything revolves around us and it is not for our sole benefit that everything has been created – after all, in one of the Genesis creation stories we were created last. All was deemed to be 'good' *before* we came along!

To grasp this will be to make a huge leap forward in opening up to and aligning ourselves with the work of the Holy Spirit – the reconciliation and healing of all creation. And, you guessed it, this is a key aspect of the work of mindfulness. Starting with the 'body scan', we begin the process of giving proper respect and attention to the sensations in (or 'messages' from) every part of the body and not just the brain; so also as we bring awareness to our thoughts we notice them not as central or controlling factors in our lives but as phenomena to be set alongside other phenomena; this leads us to be more able to see our own experiences alongside those of others; and finally, as we bring this same kind of awareness to the rest of nature, once again we learn to set our experience alongside that of every aspect of nature and so begin to see from the perspective of the whole, not just from our own. In mindfulness everything is decentred because this is the nature of reality – I am not the centre. But it takes time actually to learn this in experience. It needs practice!

The Holy Spirit is also the great democratizer. 'I will pour out my spirit on all flesh; your sons and your daughters shall prophesy, your old men shall dream dreams, and your young men shall see visions. Even on the male and female slaves, in those days, I will pour out my spirit' (Joel 2.28–29). In Acts 2 the Spirit comes to everyone and not just a chosen few. As we begin to grasp in our own experience that *every* person and *every* aspect of creation is of concern to the Holy Spirit, perhaps we can consider letting go of our 'me'-centred approach to life with our tendency towards centralized hierarchical controls, decentring our consciousness and allowing the Spirit to work through the whole of creation.

Part 3

FROM DOING TO BEING

---·◆·---

I noted in the introduction to Part 2 that people sometimes come up to me and confess that they are not sure they believe what they are supposed to. I don't get many people saying that they don't *do* what they feel they are supposed to. Plenty of people tell me that someone *else* is not doing what they are supposed to – and also that *I* am not doing what I am supposed to! And there is occasionally a reference to the inability to do anything different, because 'that is human nature, isn't it'. This last comes closest, perhaps, to how many people feel. We have a vague sense of what is required, and the vicar might try to drop a hint from time to time, but basically we all feel somewhat at the mercy of something called 'human nature' that just takes its course whatever we try and do.

Perhaps the problem is the assumption that the only way in is to tackle the 'doing' head on. Habits are incredibly difficult to change, particularly because there is very often a mental habit lurking behind a physical habit. The physical habit is kept firmly in place because of the much-harder-to-get-at mental habit that lies behind it.

Mindfulness offers us a different way of approaching things, by suggesting that it is not the doing we need to start with but the being. Jon Kabat-Zinn describes two modes of mind: 'doing' mode and 'being' mode. When the mind is in 'doing' mode it is concerned with analysing situations, getting tasks done, planning for the future and organizing. There is a feeling here of 'should', 'ought' and 'must' in the mind. There doesn't seem to be much choice in this mode because the mind is locked into a course of what needs to be done. There is also a sense of self-evidence: it quite clearly needs to be done because, well, it just needs to be done: human nature – and nothing changes.

The 'being' mode is marked by a greater and wider awareness of the present moment and a sense of opening up space to see more clearly the true nature of what is before us. There is less of a drive to do, to fix, to plan and much more of a sense of curious interest, of judgements being reserved, and of the situation being allowed to remain as it is, just for the moment, until things become clearer and the various possibilities become apparent. We are back to Mary and Martha again. Yes, if they were all going to eat that evening someone would need to do some cooking. But did it need to be done now? Was there, perhaps, something else more important going on? Was a takeaway from Mary's brother-in-law's new place later in the evening a possibility?

It is in this 'being' mode that we make space for God because this is where the choices become apparent. God is, of course, involved in both being and doing, but if we want to know what the wise and Godly thing to be doing might be, it will often be in the 'being' mode that we become aware of this. This is also the place of flexibility and openness where God might have half a chance of affecting our decisions.

In the *Frantic World* book, Mark Williams and Danny Penman reflect on seven aspects of both the 'doing' and the 'being' modes based on the important theoretical work done by Segal, Williams and Teasdale in their earlier clinical work with those vulnerable to depression. I won't rehearse them here but I want to introduce the concept because each of the following chapters, in their very different ways, will explore one way of shifting from doing to being so as to be better able to be open to God's work in our lives.

7

Knowing God's presence

A good starting point for having the confidence to 'just be', we might say, is to know that God is 'just being' here with me. So, here I am, ready to write and my mind is all over the place (again): replaying a conversation I had earlier in the day, thinking about what I might have for lunch, drifting and dreaming. Where is God? Why isn't God here with me helping me to write?

The answer, of course, is obvious when we put it like that. God is here – but I am not. And as we have already seen, God is always here but only here *now*. It is no good trying to book an appointment to see God tomorrow morning at 11.30. The divine watch will no doubt be removed from the divine pocket and after a cursory glance God will say something like, 'Mmm, so what are you doing now? It so happens that I am free!' But oh no, I am not free. I am not here now at all but am busy with many things in the past and in the future. I am thinking about what I am going to do this afternoon and wondering what the weather will be like and any number of important matters. I do not have time for God now. But I think I might be able to create some space tomorrow morning at 11.30 (maybe!).

The idea of a sense or experience of God's presence can be difficult for some Christians. If people have had a powerful sense of God's presence in the past they may look to this as a defining moment. Others can feel a bit bereft, having never felt they have experienced God in this way; they may find meaning in thoughts about God rather than in experiences of God. But whether one has felt a sense of God in the past or has profound thoughts about God now matters little if one is not experiencing God's presence in the here and now. As the evangelist J. John once said: 'I'm not talking about "pie in the sky when you die". I'm talking about "steak on the plate while you wait"!' What a great one-liner (unless you are a vegetarian). It's all about here and now and if we are not experiencing God's presence with us now, then we are not experiencing God's presence at all.

The clue is in the word 'presence'. God is only and will only ever be in the present moment for us. 'The right time has come – the kingdom of God is near', Jesus said. 'Do not worry about tomorrow.' 'Give us this day our daily bread.' The emphasis each time is on the here and now. It is in this moment that we may experience God and in no other. And according the *Frantic World* scheme, it is also through learning to be in this moment that we experience more of the 'being' mode.

Why do we find this so hard? Why do we seem to 'prefer' to be somewhere else in our minds so much of the time? I put 'prefer' in inverted commas because it doesn't seem as though we choose this, rather it just happens. What is going on? Well, perhaps there are a number of reasons.

An obvious one is that the present moment may not be all that pleasant. It could be just a little bit uncomfortable or even downright scary. We have, perhaps, mistakenly assumed that God's presence will only ever be peaceful, calm and pleasant. But this is not necessarily true. Certainly Jesus' presence was often extremely uncomfortable, and at times dangerous for the disciples. As Lucy says to her friend Mr Beaver in *The Lion, the Witch and the Wardrobe*, when she first sees the great lion Aslan: 'Is he safe?' To which Mr Beaver replies: 'Oh, no. Who said anything about safe? But he's good.'[16] God's presence may not be pleasant or safe. But it will always be good. However, our instinct, unless we can learn another way, will be to avoid or drift away from the unpleasant or scary (like the business of starting to write the next chapter, though I appear to have got over that one now) and find more pleasant thoughts or ideas to engage with.

Another reason why we may find it difficult to be present to our actual experience right now is our human tendency to intellectualize so much of the time. Give me a couple of grams of present moment experience and I am off in my head with several kilos of analysing it rather than actually experiencing it. The human mind has an enormous capacity for analysis, which has actually served us well in so many ways. But this can be just another way of avoiding the present moment – especially if the present moment is uncomfortable. One trick of the mind is to set the present experience within a narrative interpretation of our own ongoing experiences, moving from the distant past to the distant future. In this way I seek to give meaning to the present by comparing it with similar situations in the past, or my hopes to have either more or less of such experiences in the future. Some time ago my wife and I realized that whenever we came to a new place that we liked, on a walk or on a holiday, we would immediately say, 'We must come here again,' or 'How come we have never been here before?' Actually we still say it! But it is now a joke that takes us into experiencing the moment for what it is – a moment that by definition has never happened before and can never, ever happen again. It may look like many other similar experiences but it is not any other experience. It is *this* experience. And if I am seeking to know God's presence with me, then I need to look to *this* moment and *this* experience because this is where God is for me right now. If I can just find a way to be fully present to this moment, then I have a date – with God.

Another question might come: do we actually want to know God's presence? Or do we want to have a particular experience of our own choosing? You'll have heard the joke about the man whose small boat capsized and who prayed to God to come and save him. Another boat, the lifeguard ship and then a helicopter all came along but he sent them away, confident that

God would answer his prayer. He sank and died and went to heaven, then asked God sulkily whether God had been too busy at the time to come and save him. To which God replied: 'I sent two boats and a helicopter – what more did you want?' I think this is where I fall. I have had plenty of pleasant experiences in life and a few unpleasant ones – and I want more of the pleasant ones, please. That's what God is for, isn't that right? But no, apparently God is God and God comes to us as goodness, truth and beauty whether that is pleasant or not for us at the time, and we, if we want to know God, need to learn to be open to however God comes.

But, as in each of these chapters, the question will be: 'But how?' We know we need to learn to be more open and present to the here and now so that we might know God with us, but how do we do this? And how might mindfulness help?

One of the first practices we learn in the course is the 'body scan'. Here is a glimpse of what the body scan is about.

The 'sole sensation' practice

As you sit here (and you can probably carry on reading during this practice), bring your awareness to your own breath. Just start noticing your breathing. As ever, this is not about how the breathing is today – fast, slow, deep or shallow – but about being aware of it, bringing our attention to it. And the obvious way to bring attention to the breath is to notice the movements, large or small, of the body as the breath enters and leaves of its own accord. The most obvious movements tend to be around the chest and the abdomen. So, just spend a few moments with your attention on the breath, sensing its motion and rhythm. Then, when you feel ready, allow your attention to shift down through your body to the soles of your feet and see if you notice any sensations there. I have no shoes on today and can feel the softness of the carpet under my feet and the sense of the weight of my lower legs pressing downwards creating a sense of pressure. There is also a tiny amount of tingling in different parts of the sole. Right now it is clearest around the balls of both feet. I don't know what you are noticing, but I am having a ball here! – noticing stuff I never really take any notice of at all. On the other hand, you may feel you have no sensation in the soles of your feet today. In which case nothing is lost because the point is not *what* we notice but *that* we notice. Noticing absence is just as meaningful as noticing presence. Sensations can change over time too, so you may want to keep your attention here with the sole just to see what happens. Then, when you feel you have had enough, finish this practice and read on.

In the body scan proper we start roughly like this, then carry on, moving our attention slowly from one part of the body to the next in order to explore the sensations in the body. Usually we do this practice lying down on a mat or on the bed and allow the guide (or CD) to lead us through the various stages. Techniques about use of the breath can help us both to direct our attention to a particular part of the body and to let go of that part in our awareness before moving on to another part. But the main thing is this simple (but, once again, very difficult) practice of moving our attention around the body and becoming tuned in to the sensations that are present here.

Now, you may be thinking that this does not seem like a very spiritual activity! But let me suggest how this practice may be able to help with our tuning in to the presence of God.

What tends to be most people's experience when they first try this practice (which can last anything from 15 to 40 minutes) is that they become aware of just how 'un-present' they are in their minds. Virtually everyone will comment that it was not long before their minds began to wander off to all sorts of other matters that perhaps seemed more interesting or urgent than the sensations in the sole of the foot. These range from planning the rest of the day or evening, recalling events or conversations from earlier in the day and various other memories or images, to experiencing worries or anxieties about the future; or just drifting or dreaming. Some of these mind-wanderings can be pleasant, tempting us to stay with them; or they can be unpleasant, causing us to try to get rid of them, which means we usually think harder about them in order to attempt to solve or resolve whatever it is. In any case we can find ourselves rather a long way from this room and the sensations of our own bodies, and when we suddenly hear the guide or CD say, 'And now move your attention to your shoulders', we wonder, how did we get there? The last I heard we were still on the left ankle! One teacher I trained under declared that it was months before she realized that the body scan did indeed cover all the various limbs, including those between the left knee and the neck.

Some members of my youth group came to a body scan session I was leading at the Greenbelt Christian arts and music festival one year. Afterwards when I asked how they got on, all three declared themselves to have enjoyed it but then got into a discussion about what part of the body each fell asleep at. For one it was the left ankle, another the right knee and the third (proudly) made it as far as the right hip. After that it was all blissful sleep. Now, the difficult thing at this point is to help participants to let go of their self-judging and their competitive spirits and simply to give value to what they have noticed. And noticing how much the mind wanders away from the present moment experience is the absolutely vital first step in becoming more mindful. We don't become more mindful by competing and trying harder but, in the first place, by noticing how apparently un-mindful we are – which, itself, is being mindful. Got it?!

In my case, having begun to recognize how much of the time my mind is not present to the experiences I am having moment by moment, I then persevere with this as a practice and this leads to three really important things.

One is that because the body will only ever be here in the present moment, as I practise tuning in to its sensations moment by moment I am actually practising the skill of being here in the present moment. This is quite simply a skill of the mind, which takes time to learn; for so long we have simply allowed our minds free rein to be absent (in the past or in the future) whenever they want to be. But learning this skill, I suggest, is a key part of tuning into God – who is only ever here in the 'now'.

The second is illustrated by the woman I mentioned in Chapter 5 who wanted to know what God had to do with her right knee. The only way we will ever experience God is through our own senses – there is no other place we humans can be other than in the material world, experiencing things through our senses. If God wants to communicate with us, reassure us, disturb us, bring conviction or guide us, it will be through the senses in our bodies (and I include in this the thoughts in our minds), so getting better attuned to our bodies and the sensations we find there will, again, be a key part of being present to God.

Third, during the body scan it is common to notice unpleasant sensations we would rather not feel or experience at all, thank you very much. This is where the right knee really comes into play if that is where I am experiencing pain, because in mindfulness our approach is to be as fully present as possible to all sensations whether they are pleasant or not. And this serves as very good practice if I want to be present to God even if that presence is uncomfortable for me at times.

So, practising being more present in our minds to this present moment, better tuned in to our own body sensations and learning to stay present even if the experience is less than pleasant are all key ways in which we can open ourselves up to the experience of 'God with us'.

Let me finish this chapter with what has always been a very powerful story for me, about Corrie Ten Boom, whose family sheltered refugee Jews in Nazi-occupied Holland in the Second World War.[17] She was worried how she would cope if they were caught and sent to a concentration camp. Her father sympathized deeply and explained that God would help them. But, Corrie protested, the very thought of it filled her with fear and apprehension. Her father answered by reminding her that when she was a child and he took her to the train station to go to school, did she have the ticket in her hand? No, she said, he only gave her the ticket just as she was about to get on the train. 'And so it will be if we ever get caught', he said. 'We do not need the ticket right now but when the time comes God will be with us and will give us more than we need to live with what comes our way.'

God is not present to us tomorrow. God is not present to us yesterday. God is only ever present to us today. But when tomorrow comes, that will be the present and God will be there too. Let us make sure, though, that we, too, are present when tomorrow comes.

8

Trusting God

Experiencing God's presence is not only about being in the present and being tuned in to our senses. It is also about trust. We are supposed to trust God. But what does this mean and how do we do this?

You may be one of those who have been exhorted at some stage to 'trust in the Lord' in the midst of a troublesome situation. But there can be several problems with how we respond to this exhortation. One question might simply be, 'Does this mean I just do nothing?' In other words, is trust about passivity? And this is important to reflect on, since Christian spirituality can sound dangerously passive if we are not careful. Responding to some difficulty simply by accepting that this must be God's will may sound like trust but, of course, can also be a way of avoiding doing what God would have us do – for instance, standing against an injustice or making renewed efforts to make sure a particular kind of suffering does not happen again. So no, it does not mean just doing nothing; what I think it should mean is learning the way of doing those things that express our trust rather than our fear or our greed. But the other question, or statement, might be: 'But I can't trust! How do I trust?' I often feel a degree of sympathy for the people of Nazareth in Mark 6, where Jesus was not able to perform any miracles because of their lack of faith. It was difficult for them – they had known Jesus since he was (perhaps) a naughty boy chasing round the streets with a runny nose. How were they suddenly to accept him as the Messiah? How could they just 'let go' of their ingrained image of Jesus and accept a wholly new one?

And so here is the phrase that catches me when I reflect on what it means to trust: 'letting go'. It could be argued that the primary dynamic of Christian spirituality is one of letting go, particularly letting go of all that we might be clinging to out of fear and greed. Jesus let go of equality with God (Philippians 2) and all the glory and status that went with it in order to become human, 'taking the form of a slave'. Then, once human, he let go of wealth, security, a secure home and the comforts of family, so that he could follow his calling. At the Last Supper he let go even of the status he had among his own disciples in order to make sure everyone had clean feet for supper. During his trial he let go of his reputation by refusing a right to defence. And finally he let go of life itself – the ultimate expression of trust in a God he believed was greater than any one person's life. Then, and only then, was Jesus raised, by the God he had placed his trust in, to an altogether different quality of life – what we call 'resurrection life'. The only way to this kind of life is by the kind of trust in God that is marked by a persistent letting go of another kind of life that is ruled and ordered by our own fears and greed. We may feel safer in such a life but it is not resurrection life. It is not the authentic, liberating 'life in all its fullness' that Jesus promised us.

But let us go back to the first question, which now has a different phrasing: 'How do I let go of stuff?' And this question may well have quite a powerful emotional tone if you have ever found yourself just a little obsessed by a particular matter and been told by someone to 'just let it go'! The answer to this is (in capitals because, yes, I am shouting): 'I WOULD LET IT GO IF I COULD LET IT GO BUT I CAN'T LET IT GO!!!' The trouble is that we don't actually say this at all because this appears to be an admission of defeat or lack of faith. So instead we go quiet, perhaps only muttering under our breath but pretending to accept the advice.

Can mindfulness help with this? (A rhetorical question, of course, because you will have worked out by now that in this book, whatever the question, mindfulness is always the answer!)

First is the matter of a growing awareness of who is doing the clinging. This is quite a difficult one because if I am in the grip of an obsession, addiction or unhelpful habit, I can very easily become seduced by the sense that something is clinging to me and I am powerless to get rid of it. I wonder sometimes whether this kind of experience is what is behind my sense of being in the grip of evil or the devil. For some it can certainly seem like this because of the feeling of powerlessness – that is, I would change this habit if I had the choice, therefore it must be something else doing the clinging and disabling me. Simply to contradict this statement and tell me that I am the one doing the clinging may not be very helpful until I have begun to experience the truth of it for myself. This goes back to the thought explored in Chapter 6, that we actually have free will but because through our repeated habits the place of freedom and true choice has been buried, perhaps quite deep in the unconscious, I have very little perception of it and even less access to it. Instead, my daily perceived experience is that I have very little choice. But as I become increasingly self-aware I may well come to accept that it is indeed me who is doing the clinging – driven, in so many ways, by the two things I keep mentioning: my own fear and my own greed.

In my mindfulness practice this process of awareness happens through gradually becoming aware of the things my mind is repeatedly drawn to when I am intending to bring my focus to the breath, or the body, whatever I am aiming to focus on at the time. At some point – quickly or otherwise – I realize that behind each of these mini obsessions is, indeed, some form of either greed or fear. I will try hard to tell myself another story but nothing will actually start shifting until I come to recognize my own part in what is happening. So, simply to become aware of how these things are operating in my life is a very powerful first step in the letting-go process.

But how does the process of letting go actually work? Well, it is important to realize that we won't find ourselves able to let go of fear or greed by confronting them and focusing on them, nor is there is a magic formula we can say to get rid of them. Some will be deeply ingrained and what we normally find is that if we focus on the things we feel ourselves to be in the grip of (but, in fact, we are gripping on to, remember?), we just give them more power and energy. So a different strategy is called for here, and that is to acknowledge them and, well, just to let them be there. You see, we will never actually get rid of our fears or our greed and so it is hopeless to try. But we can change our relationship with them. Once they have come to the surface we can practise letting them be there and not bothering too much about them until they gradually have less and less sway over our lives.

Once again, this is not easy and needs to be worked at. There are a number of mindfulness practices that can help with this. In the body scan it is just as important that we practise letting go of one body part in our awareness as it is that we then focus on the next part. This constant letting go is another skill of the mind that needs practice. This is different from suppression – which also never works – because it is preceded by full acknowledge-ment of what is actually there. Then the mind simply moves on, or lets go of focusing on that one thing. Similarly, when we use the breath as a focus for our attention, as mentioned pre-viously, it is a universal experience that our minds are drawn away very quickly to more interesting things. The instruction is always, when we notice this, simply to acknowledge where the mind has wandered to and bring the attention gently back to the breath, which is where we intended it to be. This, again, is a form of letting go. We notice and we let go, over and over again, until it becomes a habit.

A fuller practice, which occurs later in the course, is when we deliberately turn our attention towards our thoughts and thought patterns, but in a particular way. This is not about finally allowing ourselves to drift with whatever emerges, but involves setting ourselves up, as we say, as if in front of a cinema screen ready to watch the thoughts go by. When we notice a thought we simply observe, 'Ah, there is a thought'; instead of getting caught up in the thought, engaging with it, solving it or doing battle with it, we just note that it is a mental event happening in the mind and we let it arise and pass in its own time. What is interesting about this practice is that it can be quite difficult to notice thoughts at all because of our habit of jumping into the thought and engaging with it. When we are in something, identified with it, we can't see it for what it is. It is only when we have found a place from which to watch it that we can see something for what it is. Then we see the thought as just a thought and let it pass by. Here, then, is a further form of letting go. We neither repress these thoughts nor engage with them, but note their presence and let them go on their way. And what seems to happen is that these thoughts gradually have less and less hold – less and less control – over us. We can't trust God while we are still clinging to something out of fear or greed, so we practise letting go and we find our capacity to trust God gradually grows.

The film *A Beautiful Mind* is about the brilliant mathematician John Nash, who suffered from schizophrenic hallucinations.[18] He was plagued by the presence of human figures, which were projections of his mind but to him were as real as any other person in his life. In his earlier adult years they disturbed him deeply, as he fought and argued with them. Towards the end of the film, though, there is a very moving scene where he is working at a table in his garden when these three figures appear at the end of the garden. He looks up, sees them standing there, acknowledges them and simply returns to his work. The figures look at one another, shrug and wander off. This is a sign of his growing stability, even though he would probably still be labelled 'schizophrenic'. The figures, just like our own thoughts, fears and greed, may always be there, but it is possible for us to develop the ability to let them go if we choose, so that we are no longer controlled by them.

But we need to go back to the question: 'Is that it? Do I just do nothing? Is trusting God simply about letting it all happen?' Well, as I suggested before, this is very different from passivity. There may well be some action that is either necessary or good to do, but if we develop the ability to trust God by practising the art of letting go, then we will find we have more choices because we are less in the grip of and controlled by our fear or greed. But also we will find we come to see more clearly what actions are born out of our fears and what actions genuinely come from trust and faith.

Finally in this chapter, there is one very important subject that will plague us all at times. And I am indebted to a participant at one of our Greenbelt sessions who, after I had been speaking about this subject, suggested a link with a talk we had all heard earlier in the day by Mpho Tutu. It was about her book *The Book of Forgiving*, written with her father Desmond Tutu.[19] They recount the fourfold path of forgiving: telling the story, naming the hurt, granting forgiveness and renewing or releasing the relationship.

Might it be possible, this woman suggested, that the skill I had described of letting go could be a fifth thread here? I am naturally very cautious of this, since to suggest to someone who has been deeply wounded, abused or oppressed by another that they should 'let it go' would rightly be seen as the most appallingly insensitive response, giving no regard for the depth of wounding and emotional scarring that has been suffered. On the other hand, if having engaged fully with the four stages of the Tutus' understanding of the process of authentic forgiveness, someone genuinely wanted no longer to be plagued by images and memories that now served no useful purpose, then could this sort of practice come into play to assist with this final stage? I cannot conceive of being able to speak for those who have suffered the kind of abuse the Tutus witnessed; but it is the approach I try to follow in my own life when a perceived wrong is in the past and has been dealt with in all the appropriate ways yet still keeps coming to mind, churning me up and shifting a perfectly decent mood into one of combative anger! What I try to do now is what John Nash was depicted doing in the film. I take note that that old wound is still there, and just allow it to be there without engaging with it. And what seems to happen is that such thoughts gradually reduce in their intensity until I hardly notice them. Yes, perhaps it is time that heals these things, but this does not always happen, and it may be that we can be helped by gradually learning the skill of letting go. Otherwise, if we continue to cling, to engage and constantly to do battle, time may not heal. Time may even do exactly the opposite.

Letting go, then, may be possible after all, and may well have a very full part to play in both forgiving and in learning to trust God.

9

Knowing God's will

In the previous chapter I suggested that trusting God was not necessarily about doing nothing (though sometimes it might be). This leads on to the question, 'If there is something I should be doing as a response to this trust, how do I know what it is?' How can we know God's will?

This is something of a thorny one, because the concept can be easily abused and manipulated by those who may claim special knowledge, and it can be somewhat bewildering for those who don't. Various kinds of 'tests' are available to decide what may or may not be God's will, such as the guidance of Scripture, the norms of the Church and the reflections of wise friends. But these are not absolute: our understanding of Scripture is both developing and not always easy to interpret; the Church admits that it has been wrong at times; and Job will be the first to tell you that supposedly wise friends are not always reliable. What happens when we come down to a choice of two or three options, all of which are moral, are not opposed by Scripture and could be considered Godly in some way? How do I know whether the choice I am leaning towards is God's will, or my own will, which I happen to have found a few choice Scripture texts to support?

One of my favourite stories on this subject concerns an ordinand (priest in training) who was required to go on a three-day retreat leading up to his ordination. The retreat took place in the bishop's house and gardens, which were entirely walled in. The only exit was through the bishop's front door, which was next to the bishop's study. One afternoon the bishop was walking in the garden and found this ordinand in the act of climbing over the garden wall. The bishop needed to do no more than raise an eyebrow for the ordinand to blurt out in his own defence: 'Excuse me, bishop, but it seemed a good idea to me and the Holy Spirit that I should go shopping this afternoon.' To which the bishop replied, hardly batting an eyelid, 'Well, it's strange you should both be wrong because it's early closing this afternoon!' (For the younger generation, once upon a time all shops closed at lunchtime on one day a week. This was called 'early closing'!)

The endless and often fruitless quest for who is right about God's will leads me to wonder whether we need to reframe the question in terms of what constitutes wisdom and how we grow in it, such that when the time comes we will simply know what is right – or at least, we will gradually get better at knowing. Compare the story above with that of Elijah on Mount Carmel.

In 1 Kings 19, Elijah is in a deep quandary and he needs to know God's will. God takes him to the top of the mountain and tells him to stand there. There then passes by a furious wind, then there is an earthquake and then a fire, but God is not in any of these dramatic and noisy events. Elijah seems to know this, and so he continues to wait until he hears 'a still small voice' (AV) or 'a sound of sheer silence' (NRSV). And then he knows that this is the voice of the Lord, which subsequently speaks to him and opens up his future. But how did he know? God seems to speak through all sorts of natural phenomena in the Bible, and at Pentecost God was most certainly in the fire *and* in the wind. So how did Elijah know that this fire and this wind did not contain the voice of God for him?

The problem for us is that there are so many voices around. For me most of them are my own inner voices, coming from various places within, of longing, desire, fear and fantasy. Some of them belong to my mother or my father, from my very early days, telling me that this is right and that is wrong, I should be ashamed of this and I should be achieving that – by my age!

Pretty much all the voices can be divided up into expressions of, on the one hand, desire (things I want more of) and, on the other, aversion (things I want less of). And these voices can be very compelling – as loud as winds, fires and earthquakes – so no wonder they can get in the way of our hearing clearly the authentic 'still small voice' of God. Added to this is the fact that we are often not even fully aware of our desires and aversions. We may have learned from an early age that certain desires were shameful or certain aversions were 'inappropriate' and so have buried them to the extent we are hardly conscious of them. And yet they will still be at work, affecting our hearing.

Knowing God's will, then, with this interpretation of seeking wisdom, begins with our becoming more fully aware of our own wills in the form of our desires and aversions. If we could see what these are more clearly, then perhaps we would have half a chance of discerning the authentic from the froth. And this is the part that mindfulness can help with.

The practice I described in the last chapter is a difficult one to get the hang of but is a fundamental and enormously valuable skill, so I shall attempt to dig a little deeper here. The practice is normally taught in week five or six, when we have been working at the 'focus' practices for some time.

It is necessary to develop at least a familiarity with the idea of an 'anchor' before we begin to engage with this practice. The anchor is any focus for our attention that is most definitely in the present moment and in this space; it is usually our breath or some part of our body. So, this practice starts with focus on the breath. As ever, we very quickly notice the mind wandering, thinking about other matters, getting caught up with mental images, or just daydreaming. In order to establish the breath as the anchor, we stay with it as far as is possible, repeatedly returning to the breath every time the mind wanders off.

The next stage of this practice is interesting and usually one of the more pleasant ones as we shift our attention first to a sense of the whole body and then to the sounds that may be around. With sounds we are beginning to practise a certain kind of attention that we will shortly use when we come to turn our attention to our thoughts. When we listen to sounds we are seeing if we can hear them just for their pitch, timbre, tone and duration, not for any meaning or narrative behind them. We may like or not like certain sounds but that is of no concern here. All we want to do at this point is hear – there is no need for our conscious rational storytelling minds to get involved. Of course, they will anyway – so as soon as we notice that our minds have been triggered into thinking about a sound, telling the story behind it or even drifting off down a train of thought triggered by the sound, we see if we can come back to just hearing the sounds for themselves.

Finally in this practice we turn our attention towards the thoughts themselves. And the aim here is to see if we can bring the same quality of attention to the thoughts as we brought to the sounds. Is it possible just to 'hear' the thoughts as thoughts, in the same way that we heard the sounds – as if they were just mental events happening in the mind and without getting caught up with them, responding to them, fixing them, analysing them or judging them? Can we let the thoughts be thoughts, just as we let the sounds simply be sounds? Well, once again, 'no' is usually the answer! Usually one of the following happens instead.

For many of us, strangely, the moment we actually turn our attention towards the thoughts that have been bothering us all along, while we have been trying to focus on something else, they disappear completely! Just like bugs in the night when you shine a torch on them. Gone! Nothing! It can be very disconcerting when this first happens. But when I began to understand that perhaps, for possibly very good reasons, my thoughts are a little bit shy and do not want to be looked at directly, I found myself able to bring more of a gentle compassionate approach to paying attention to them. Thoughts particularly do not want to show themselves if they think they are going to be judged harshly. So this non-judging approach is very important. We need to approach with the acceptance that whatever is here in the mind is already here, so there is no point in scolding myself for having this hateful thought or that distressing image. Much better that I am aware that these thoughts are around in my mind – then I may be better able to deal with them.

Another very common experience is that by the time we become aware of our thoughts we have already been caught up in a train of thoughts that has been going on for some time. I may even wonder how I got here, but the point is that I have and so I simply 'get off the train' of thoughts and, as it were, come back to the station, waiting to notice any other thoughts arise. Occasionally a thought arises that I find overwhelming or distressing, and I may at this stage choose to opt out by returning to the anchor of my breath – which is allowed, by the way! It is important to be gentle with ourselves and to feel we have a choice.

Gradually, I may begin to experience the thoughts coming and going in my mind without engaging with them or getting carried away with them. And this is when I can start to affirm a key notion in mindfulness that is one of the key characteristics of the 'being' mode: that thoughts are not facts, they are just thoughts, 'mental events'. A particular thought may be true or it may not – so it is a thought, not a fact. The thought, if I can catch it, that this book I am writing is going to be a classic is no more or less true than the thought I had yesterday that it was doomed to failure and who was I kidding. (It's my first book – I'm allowed such fluctuations!) The thought that my wife is irritated with me because I bought too much food again; the thought that this song I have written is really rather good; the thought that I am right about a certain matter in the parish or the thought that I am wrong; the thought that that was a cracking sermon; or that, 'truth' be told, my career has plateaued – all these are just thoughts. At the time of appearing in my own mind, they have no more claim on factual accuracy than any other thought. The most compelling ones may have a grain of truth – which is why they are compelling – but they are *still* just thoughts.

So, when I finally get the hang of this idea I may begin to apply the same principle to the desires and aversions that lie behind them. When a strong desire arises, perhaps in the form of an image or an idea or even a narrative, I am in a better position (because I have been practising) to recognize this as a desire – something I would really like to have or to do. And because I have also practised bringing a non-judging awareness to this desire, I don't praise or condemn myself for having this desire; I just take note of it. It becomes a thing of genuine interest to me. 'Ooh, I didn't realize quite how much I wanted this or that outcome in my work or in my personal life. But here is this longing popping up in my mind over and over again.' Or, 'I hadn't realized how much I dislike those people, but every time they come to mind I find I am tensing up – how *interesting*!' Note that it is not 'how awful of me' but simply 'how interesting'. We need to acknowledge that we have little control over what pops up in the mind, so this is not awful. What would be awful is if, completely unaware of my prejudice, I persistently excluded or avoided the person concerned.

So here we are becoming gradually more aware of the noise of our own true desires and aversions (our furious winds, fires and earthquakes), and we are practising, just like Elijah, simply watching them and letting them pass. The desires and aversions are still there but we are less controlled by them. We become increasingly able to take them or leave them. In other words, we have choice again. In the 'desert' tradition of the early Church fathers and mothers this was known as *apatheia*, which is not served well by its similarity to our word 'apathy' but is best translated as 'disinterest'. It is a state in which we are aware of our desires, and in fact even experience them more fully, but have learned the skill of no longer being compelled to fulfil them.

Quite simply, this seems to be how our desires begin to lose their intensity so that we can become more sensitized to the often quieter, more persistent voice of God saying 'This way' or 'That way is the way for you'. And when we begin to hear this voice, we sense its authenticity and we wonder why we have not heard it before – it is like coming home.

So, once we have become more fully aware of our own will, we have a greater chance of discerning God's will – the 'still small voice' of authenticity and truth. This, then, is the beginning of wisdom.

10

Finding peace

We may feel that we are beginning to know God's presence and also to discern God's will, but what about when we are in turmoil, when life's circumstances have just overwhelmed us? How do we find peace in the midst of our suffering?

'Thank God for your faith, Jack. Where would you be without that?' So says the well-meaning chaplain to C. S. Lewis in the play *Shadowlands*, after his wife's funeral. To which Lewis replies: 'I'm sorry, Harry, but it won't do. This is a mess, and that's all there is to it.'[20]

We are supposed, it seems, as Christians, to have the key to being peaceful even in the most traumatic situations. Coming across as flustered, angry or deflated may be seen by some as a sign of lack of faith, or that our faith doesn't work very well. After all, don't we know that everything is going to be all right because God is looking after us? Don't we have Christ within us who is the Prince of Peace? But for many of us – perhaps most of us – this is often not our experience. Flustered, angry, upset, afraid, anxious, irritated and any amount of 'inappropriate' behaviour – all have been part of our experience at one time or another. The particular difficulty for Christians (and I am even more acutely aware of it now I'm supposed to be a mindfulness teacher!) is that because we know we are supposed to be able to remain calm we are tempted to act that way on the outside while we feeling anything but peaceful within. Gradually we can end up, if we are not careful, repressing the turmoil rather than dealing with it, which can cause even more problems.

So, my starting point would be to suggest that, as Christians, as Lewis so wonderfully demonstrated, we need to learn to be more honest about our experiences. If circumstances seem inexplicable to us and throw us into turmoil, then perhaps we need simply to admit to this. Honesty and integrity, I would like to suggest, are greater attributes than the ability to remain calm in all circumstances; it is important to realize that Christians (and mindfulness teachers) experience the same pressures as everyone else. And yet a number of very powerful and moving stories in the Gospels seem to imply that peace in the midst of the storm is something that we can experience in Christ.

Most explicitly there is the story of Jesus calming the storm in Mark 4.35–41. There appear to me to be two important contrasting parts to this story. The first describes how Jesus seems to be so calm in the midst of this particular storm that it doesn't even disturb his sleep. In the second part, he recognizes that the disciples are being overwhelmed not just with water but with panic, and he calms the storm. The first part is about being peaceful despite the circumstances and the second is about bringing peace by changing the circumstances. Which of these to expect or to pray for will depend on our situation, but what is clear is that the circumstances cannot always be changed. Indeed, the most profound narrative in the Gospels involves adverse circumstances that cannot be changed – certainly not if Jesus is going to fulfil his calling – and that is the Passion itself. Faced with the most appalling fear from within and real-life horror from without, Jesus is shown to remain calm, quiet and entirely dignified. He clearly knew the terror of it all, as any human would, as depicted in the graphic scene in Gethsemane. But even here was a sense that somewhere, somehow, he knew a deeper peace, which held him through the turmoil of his awful experience that night.

Can anyone know this kind of peace? Or is it, let's be honest, just for those who have a certain type of personality or who were brought up in a particular way? Well, it would seem that some people do have a head start in all this, but as one who is probably not one of those, I do feel that mindfulness has helped me grow in this area.

The key text, for me, is found in Luke 5.1–8, when Peter first encounters Jesus. Peter is such a wonderful model for us because he is so honest and does not appear to hide his inner conflicts. So when he has been invited to push his boat out into 'deep water' and they catch a huge haul of fish (having caught nothing all night), Peter falls on his knees and says two significant things: 'Go away from me, Lord' and 'for I am a sinful man!' The first is particularly interesting because you might have expected Peter, in a polished Gospel text, to offer words of admiration and praise for Jesus. But instead he finds he wants to push Jesus away. For me, this is an indication that it was Peter who actually got the point. Something rather extraordinary was going on here, suggesting the presence of the divine or something similar, and he felt exposed. He was extremely uncomfortable and his reaction – like most of us – was to attempt to push away that which was making him feel uncomfortable. Unlike most of us, though, he then goes on to admit that he recognized that this was his problem rather than Jesus'. For most of us, if a circumstance or a person makes us feel uneasy, uncomfortable of downright panicky inside, it is *their* fault; so it is fully justified that we want to push the person or circumstance away. Or if we can't push it away we feel fully justified in avoiding it or them.

In mindfulness we call this 'avoidance'. We start by recognizing that it is a common human instinct. There are very good reasons why we appear to be hardwired to avoidance tactics, and these are mainly because in the most important situations in life they will actually save our lives. Caught in the middle of the road when a bus is coming towards you at 30 mph? Run! Find yourself in the presence of someone with a nasty cold who is coughing and sneezing? Take a step back. For evolutionists, the theory is that those of our ancestors who were most likely to run away when they saw something that looked like a snake in the path were the ones who survived and passed on their genes. Those who were more taken by the thought that it was probably a stick (nine times out of ten) were the ones who got bitten (once in ten)!

So, the emotional instinct of avoidance is very strong in us. But there are two problems with this. One is that it is not always possible to avoid or fix external circumstances: like Jesus at his Passion or C. S. Lewis after his wife's death. The other is that trying to fix or avoid inner discomfort – emotional or psychological issues, for example – in the way we try to fix other unwanted situations doesn't seem to work at all. We will either make things worse or suppress the feelings – which may seem to help in the short term but will bring more problems later. So we need another strategy, and the one that mindfulness offers us to help with this is to develop the rather counterintuitive skill of opening up to, and actually approaching rather than avoiding, that which is difficult for us. It is through approaching rather than avoiding that we find peace in the storm.

Now, as many participants have noted, this is not one of the fun bits of the course! And for many there is a huge reluctance to engage with it. So it probably needs to be said before I go into this that we need to be gentle with ourselves here. Nothing should feel forced or expected, and opting out is always possible and sometimes wise. But equally it can be a very powerful skill that will help us to engage more creatively and calmly with some of the more difficult things life will bring to us – the storms that will not be calmed.

The practice, which is a development of that described in the previous chapter, runs something like this. We would start, as ever, with a period of time focusing on the breath, then expanding the attention to the body as a whole. During this first section, whenever the attention is drawn off to thoughts elsewhere we simply note this and come back to the breath or to the body as a whole. We spend most of the time with this kind of 'focus' practice as this is what will give us the sense of rootedness or anchor that we need. The image that works for me is that of someone wanting to lean over a pool or a river to get a closer look at what is in there but not wanting to fall in. The time taken to anchor ourselves to the shore with a rope or a helping hand is important. Falling in is not the intention here, but rather remaining in touch with the anchor; just looking is quite enough to start with.

Then, at a point of our choosing (or when the CD or teacher suggests), we shift our approach. We make a conscious decision to allow into our minds some thought or image, or something real in our lives that causes us difficulty – a tension or anxiety, or a troublesome situation that is unresolved. If we have been aware of something coming up in the first part of the practice, now is the time to give it a bit of space and allow it to be there more fully. If nothing arises, then we may choose to deliberately bring to mind something that is difficult or painful. Now, this is 'practice', remember, and we are just starting out in what is not an easy skill to learn, so it may be best not to start with the most traumatic thing in your life. Best to start with something at the easier end, until we have developed the skill a bit. When learning the piano we start with middle C and the C major scale, which is the easiest because it is just the white notes. Start with B flat minor and you will become discouraged very quickly and more than likely not turn up for your second lesson. So, let's start with the scale of C when we choose our difficulty!

When we bring a difficult situation to mind we may notice the mind's usual tendencies when confronted with something it doesn't like: avoidance – wandering off to something more pleasant; analysis – trying to impose some sort of logical structure on the situation; fixing – trying to solve it in some way; judging – deciding who is at fault here; developing the narrative – playing out how we want this story to end, or how we fear it might end. But we want to see if it is possible to leave all this mind activity to one side and simply be in the presence of this difficulty and stay there. Once again, if we linger for more than a few seconds we find that it is not possible to resist our various avoidance strategies, so we have another strategy to help us to not get caught up in this compulsive thinking.

We are invited, once the situation is there in our minds, to make another deliberate shift in our attention down into the body and see if there is any corresponding sensation within the body. Whether there is or not, this is where we stay for a while, exploring the body's sensations rather than the mind's usually futile attempts to fix things. If we find no sensations we may simply move around exploring the body for any sensations for a while (just to practise this part); if there are strong or significant sensations, this is where we may choose to stay with our attention, not in order to get rid of or lessen them, but simply to practise being with them. We may choose to imagine ourselves breathing down into them in order to explore them; they may then change, or they may not, but still the point is simply to be present in the face of the difficult feelings, rather than follow the other strategies we might usually use instinctively, many of which don't really help matters.

People have all sorts of responses to this practice. I have personally found it a revelation, as at times I feel emotion very powerfully in my body. I have never known how to deal with it before and so have always sought to avoid or repress it as quickly and effectively as I can. But this has not helped either the situation or my stress levels, and has encouraged emotional habits and possibly an approach to the whole of life marked not by a sense of opening up to life but rather one of closing down and making things as safe and controlled as possible.

One participant gave herself to this practice during the week, particularly focusing on a sister she had not spoken to for a long time because of a deep family rift. Towards the end of the week she received, out of the blue, a phone call from her sister. It was a necessary call, to do with the care of their ageing parents, but the course participant said that previously she would have blanked her sister and the call would, like so many previous ones, have left them both feeling extremely negative towards one another. But on this occasion, having been spending quite a lot of time simply being with this difficult situation in her mind and practising not judging, fixing or analysing, somehow her heart was more open and the tone of the call was completely different. It felt as though there was the possibility of something new opening up for them both.

St Silouan, an Orthodox monk of Mount Athos, put it rather more starkly: 'Keep your mind in hell, and despair not'! In our mindfulness classes we often make use of the poem by Rumi called 'The Guest House'.[21] It is worth looking up and meditating upon. This quite challenging poem describes an open, approaching attitude to the whole of life, whatever comes our way.

There is a piece of artwork that I usually bring along when we do this session in the course. It is one of Stanley Spencer's series of paintings known as *Christ in the Wilderness*. The particular one I use is called 'The Scorpion',[22] and depicts the Christ figure sitting partly cross-legged in the wilderness, cradling and gazing intently at a scorpion cupped in the palm of his hand. The gaze is not one of fear but of love. This is his enemy. He would have every 'right', you might say, to run away or even to kill in order to protect himself. For all of us such a situation would elicit some deeply unpleasant feelings, ranging from fear to anger to panic. And yet, in Stanley's extraordinary vision of Christ, there is stillness, there is peace, there is love.

Many of life's circumstances cannot be avoided or explained neatly. Jesus demonstrated to us, though, that it is possible not to be overwhelmed by them. This, I think, is what we mean by 'peace' here. Not warm, inner cosy feelings but the ability to be in the storm and not panic – nor add our own anxiety and fear to what is already unpleasant enough. This mindfulness practice more than any other is the one that has helped me to discover this in my own experience.

11

'Inner healing'

———•◦•———

Following God is not just about finding peace in all circumstances. Sometimes the circumstances themselves need to be changed – and those circumstances might not be 'other people' but *us* and our inner lives. And so we come to the issue of what, in some circles, is known as 'inner healing'. I have used inverted commas here because it is probably unhelpful to separate off inner healing as if it were something different from 'outer healing'. Really there is just 'healing', involving both physical and mental processes, which in mindfulness tend to be treated as all part of the whole. However, since my own involvement in mindfulness has been focused on the areas of stress, depression and anxiety, I will tend to lean towards the emotional and psychological aspects of healing here – hence, 'inner healing'.

I would define 'inner healing' as the process by which we become as whole and as free as is possible for each of us as human beings. A Christian account of this might be described as the process by which the soul draws close to divine wholeness such that what is not whole is exposed to pure love and so is healed – or made whole. But what part does mindfulness have to play in this process?

The particular contribution mindfulness offers to the healing process is not to eliminate symptoms, or even to get rid of their causes, but to enable a change in *relationship* with those things that cause us pain or cause us to bring pain to others. The work of God, one might argue, is all about the restoring of right relationships. When Jesus healed the ten lepers it seemed to be their relationship with the community (restored through the priests) and with himself (through the thanksgiving of the one who returned) that was the real point. When Jesus healed the man lowered through the roof it was the restored relationship with God rather than the physical healing that Jesus emphasized. So it is our relationship with those things that we may feel are part of our brokenness that is important, and this is precisely where mindfulness seems to be able to help.

But before looking at mindfulness itself, we need to consider another key theological principle.

Perhaps one of the most painful taunts shouted at Jesus on the cross was, 'He saved others; he cannot save himself' (Mark 15.31), which must have been particularly galling as this could be seen as one of the key temptations that he had resisted – he could, we might think, have chosen to save himself. Instead he voluntarily chose the path that the rest of humanity has no choice but to follow – which is that we are not actually able to save ourselves.

An early theological controversy around what is known as the 'two natures' of Christ was resolved in relation to this understanding. The difficulty was how to reconcile Jesus' humanness with his divinity. Which was true and to what degree? The matter was settled (that he was both fully human and fully divine) when it was argued that he could only actually save us (or heal us) if he was both at the same time, without diminishment of either. This was based on the honest assessment of human experience that we cannot save ourselves because we have no vantage point. We are stuck in our own mire; we have no foothold with which to lever ourselves out of our situation. Yes, we needed someone who was entirely like us (otherwise he would simply be a superhuman who we could only admire but never become like), but also someone entirely not like us (who, therefore, had that vantage point from which to lift us into another way of being).

So, although this is all rather technical stuff, it is a very important concept to grasp. If we think that it is entirely up to us to heal ourselves or to effect our own salvation, we hugely diminish what might be possible for us. In Christian thought, though, there is something so much greater than our own limited understanding or capability that is available to us: the divine imagination – a vision of humanity that is way beyond our own imaginings. And the divine imagination can not only take us beyond our own limited ideas for ourselves; it is also based in the reality of what is actually possible for us.

So it is God, through the Holy Spirit, who does the healing. But does this mean that there is nothing for us to do? Do we just sit here and wait as patiently as we can (and usually not so) for the Spirit to get on with the job in hand? Well, tempting though this might be, the answer is, of course, sadly, no. God only ever works through relationships of openness and trust, and this therefore requires of us a very significant part in the process, and that is the 'giving of permission'. This is a much more profound and difficult business than simply ticking the box on a medical form. It requires the involvement of our whole selves, and more notably our whole wills. God does not want simply to perform an act on us as a surgeon might on an unconscious patient; God needs us to be co-healers – entirely involved and entirely in consent with every part of the process.

But how do we do this 'giving of permission'? Well, this links with the idea of bringing things out of the darkness and into the light referred to in Chapter 2. Jesus says in Luke 8.17, 'For nothing is hidden that will not be disclosed, nor is anything secret that will not become known and come to light.' It is hiddenness that is the problem (the shady sides of life and of the human person), not necessarily because what is hidden is bad, but often simply because it is hidden. Our work, or our 'permission-giving', involves allowing those things that are hidden in us to be brought into the light; then, and only then, the Holy Spirit can begin to help us into a new relationship with them. And this is what drawing close to the divine wholeness is all about.

Now, a quick reality check here. This is hard. In fact, very hard! The things in our lives that are currently hidden are hidden for a reason. Often they are hidden because of the shame, fear or emotional pain associated with them. They need to come to the light for healing, but if we bring up the memories or other hidden aspects of ourselves we will also bring up the feelings of shame or fear as well. And we don't like such feelings. So our unconscious minds say, 'Stay hidden – keep your heads down!' And they do.

This is where it is very important that we remember that our God is not a condemning God but a God of gentleness and mercy. Yes, God judges, but judges in order to declare us innocent! If we, perhaps even only unconsciously, have an image of God who is waiting to pounce and make us feel bad, then we are unlikely even to begin to engage in this process.

The wonderful thing is, though, that simply allowing things to come to consciousness in the presence of a loving God is healing in itself for perhaps 90 per cent of our problems, because this is what brings us into a new relationship of openness with them. Yes, we may at times feel we need further help from a confessor, psychotherapist or wise friend, but, as Crocodile Dundee famously declared, while trying to understand the American psychotherapeutic way of dealing with problems: 'If I have a problem I tell Wally, Wally tells Donk, Donk tells the rest of the village and then it is no longer a problem!'[23]

It is tempting, though, once we have become aware of some aspect of our 'stuff', to rush in and attempt to analyse it, and fix it ourselves. We humans are very good at this on the whole. Our brains have evolved to recognize what the current situation is, how we would like it to be, then let the tension created by the recognition of this difference create the energy needed to find a solution. This is known, in the trade, as 'discrepancy-based processing' (I can sense you are impressed). The trouble with this approach, though, is that not everything can be fixed in this way, especially emotional problems; in such cases this approach can be at best useless and at worst make things considerably more difficult, as we expend great amounts of energy in trying to fix something that cannot be mended. In the process we add to the tension and frustration – which then become further blocks to our healing.

The skill we need to learn instead is simply to stop at the point at which we become aware of something, then trust the Spirit to help us into this new relationship with what we find – a relationship not of judgement but of love. If there is something more we should be doing, we may become aware of this in time, but to start with we need to learn to be present, to be open and to allow what has emerged to be there and not be judged – remembering what courage it has taken to allow it to emerge at all.

How can mindfulness practice help with this? Well, first there is the constant emphasis on non-judging. We don't even need to mention God to feel judged! There is often quite enough of the judge in each of us already to more than match a false image of a harshly judging God. In mindfulness classes, it is usually one of the first things to become apparent. Even with the supposedly very simple and emotionally neutral practice of the body scan, people turn up at the next session, having had a go at home, with comments like: 'I felt I wasn't doing it right'; 'I got annoyed with myself because I didn't feel any more relaxed or peaceful'; 'I just couldn't get the hang of it'; 'My mind kept wandering off and I felt I failed completely'. Or, more subtly but still really expressing the judge (though a positive one this time): 'It worked really well for me'; 'I felt I was progressing well'. Or, indeed, the judging can be turned towards the teacher or the practice itself: 'This practice wasn't good for me'; 'The voice on the CD was so annoying'. The first task of the teacher is gently to help us start noticing how quick we are to judge ourselves or someone else against some unspoken and unacknowledged standard.

Actually, of course, the students were not sent home after the first session with the instruction to achieve any particular standard at all but simply to notice what happens – whatever we notice is simply what happens and does not require any judging. Yes, there may come a time when we make some sort of decision about how to respond to what we have noticed, but always the initial stage is to try to suspend judgement so that we become more fully aware of what is there in the first place. There may be no need for any response but only to acknowledge a part of ourselves we had not been aware of before. As soon as we become aware of the aim not to judge, though, we naturally very quickly start judging ourselves for being judging! The approach here, which seems to work eventually, is not to battle with our judging inclinations but simply to notice the judging and get used to it. Gradually the judging voice comes to have less power over us and we can get on with the business of allowing what is hidden to emerge into the light, which happens much more effectively if there is no judge around.

Having begun to get the hang of noticing the things that emerge in our minds without judging them, the mindfulness practice that is most helpful in this process of allowing God to heal us is the one described in Chapter 9: where we practise letting thoughts emerge in our consciousness without getting caught up in them. In that chapter I was talking about it in relation to the process of becoming more fully aware of our own wills, in order to have a greater chance of not confusing them with God's will. Here I want to set this practice in the much broader context of our ongoing healing and growth by persistently bringing to light that which is hidden.

This practice will help us over time as we become increasingly aware of the thoughts that emerge in our minds. And actually the really fascinating part – although it can be a bit shocking – is when we begin to notice what is actually going on in our minds. This will often not happen immediately; many people's reported early experience of mindfulness is boredom. There seems to be simply nothing going on, when we are used to an active and creative life with lots of stimulus. This was true for me. On the first short course I went on I was asked to describe my experience of the body scan, and my answer was almost always 'boredom'. But I gradually began to be aware of what was going on in my mind and I have never looked back! It's fascinating! Quite extraordinary to watch! And not all 'U' certificate material either! (Or should I be admitting that?) Totally random stuff can just emerge which you may feel has nothing to do with anything at all. Our minds can drift in endless streams of apparently trivial thoughts and images. I sometimes wonder whether this is my mind beginning to check out whether there really is a judge out there waiting to pounce, because this can go on at this level for quite some time. However, after a while (which may even mean weeks of practice) we may start to notice patterns of thoughts or persistent thoughts emerging. And very often this is precisely what has been need-ing to emerge 'into the light' so that God can bring healing.

There was an occasion when I was partway through an eight-day silent retreat when I found that one situation in my life kept coming up in my mind again and again. It was not an easy situ-ation, and when I got the chance to speak with the retreat leader and he asked how I was getting on, my answer was 'Terrible!' To which he replied, 'Well, I suppose that is par for the course on day three.' I wasn't sure whether that was supposed to be comforting, but it was reassuring that he thought nothing disastrous was going on. He went on to say that when we have more time to create space in our practice, it is a bit like digging deeper in our lives. Sometimes we hit a layer of hard rock, by which he meant something that needs a longer time and much patience before it resolves or shifts in any way.

So, here is the crucial point in the process: the involvement of the Holy Spirit. When a difficult or painful thought or emo-tion emerges there is a very strong temptation to fix it as soon as possible. We are not good at living with unresolved issues, let alone painful ones. But this is just where the mindful skill of being able to allow things simply to be present, and unresolved, is key. The Spirit can work within us no faster than we are able to do our permission-giving. Every step of the way requires our involvement and our agreement, and we give this by daring to allow something to be present in our lives with all its contradictions and discomforts. And this is what we do day by day, moment by moment in mindfulness practice – we simply allow things to emerge and choose, moment by moment, not to judge them and not to try to fix them ourselves; instead we invite the Holy Spirit to be part of the healing process in whatever way seems fit. This is how our relationship with the issue or situation can begin to change – not by getting rid of it or solving it, but by allowing it to come to the surface and meeting it not with shame or judgement but with love. We are exposing that which is not whole to the divine wholeness – divine love. It is love that heals, not judgement.

In my own case, spending that week becoming aware of a major block in my life – and I have to say it was *not* what I call fun – was enough to begin to shift it, to the extent that now I look back and say that it was the beginning of a very major healing.

A final word about the 'judge' and how its presence is so unhelpful to the process of healing. Shame is one of the great tyrants of our inner life. Very often it is not the emotion, the memory or the buried image that is the problem but the shame we have attached to it. A common, though too often unspoken, illustration of this involves sexual or aggressive thoughts. We may have a boss or supervisor we hate with all our heart, or a co-worker for whom we have sexual feelings that we are aware we should not have. Thoughts and images go round and round in the mind, never resolving, never leaving us alone despite all our efforts. A big problem with sexuality and aggression is not our desires but the shame we have managed to attach to them. We may have come from a background where we have learned that certain feelings are just plain wrong. So, when such imagery emerges in the mind, this can be a little disturbing. Now, there may well be some (or many!) such thoughts that it would be unhelpful or harmful to act out, but simply having the thought or image is not wrong in itself; it is just an illustration of how the mind and body work.

If we keep following the practice of simply allowing what is present to be here without judgement, we have a much greater chance of this whole area of our lives being brought to wholeness. Fighting with such images because of our shame never really works anyway but is more likely to repress that part of the mind's activity and so give the images more (and hidden) power. In mindfulness one might instead come to a point of open-hearted curiosity about the images that emerge in our minds when they are given the chance: 'Ah, what an interesting image my mind has concocted!' or 'How strange!' or 'I hadn't realized that was how I felt', and then leave it at that – leave it to the Holy Spirit. And what seems to happen is that such images just become less of a 'problem' to us as they are released from their associated shame and become more integrated into the rest of our being. The images may continue to emerge but we get used to them, are less driven by them and have more choice as to how to respond to them. This is the opposite of repression and is the process by which our impulses are integrated with the rest of our being and so we become more whole. And for me, this is very much a part of the process of divine healing.

Harry Williams gives us a very powerful related example of the mind breaking free from the judge and revealing what is present. In his autobiography, *Some Day I'll Find You*,[24] he describes how he sensed that a thought was wanting to emerge in his mind but found that he was unable to think it. After several days, the thought finally broke through – it was an image of God defecating through the clouds on to a cathedral! Indeed, this was truly shocking, and you can imagine why he had not wanted to think it. But it was only after he had allowed the thought to be thought that God was able to help him to engage with what was behind it, and find healing in a particular area in his life.

So, the healing process is when that which is not yet whole draws close to divine wholeness. God alone is the healer but needs our full and total cooperation. We offer this by allowing every aspect of our lives, one by one, to come to the light and holding them before the perfect gaze of God's love. The healing itself comes as we come into a new relationship with what emerges, not of judgement but of love. Mindfulness practice can help us to be able to do this.

12

Prayer and worship

———•◦•———

Let us now turn to a question that is often asked: 'Is mindfulness practice prayer?' This is important to reflect on, because it can certainly look like it. I would prefer, however, to frame it as a more nuanced question: 'What is the relationship between mindfulness and prayer?'

In my own reflections I have been keen to keep mindfulness and prayer separate for as long as possible for a number of reasons. First, this is in line with the objectives of those who developed mindfulness in mainstream contexts, in order for it to remain inclusive – in other words, so that people who have no interest in prayer or religion have access to something that can be enormously helpful in their personal lives. Second, mindfulness comes with its own insights from the world of science and from Eastern philosophy, and I am very keen that these should not be lost simply by equating the two. My starting point, therefore, would be to suggest that mindfulness is mindfulness but that it can help with prayer. Or, in the language of the theme of this book, it can make space for prayer to happen more effectively and more profoundly. I will come back to this point at the end of the chapter.

The way mindfulness supports prayer, I suggest, is in helping us to develop a certain kind, or quality, of attention. Iain McGilchrist, in his masterwork *The Master and His Emissary*,[25] describes two essential types of attention found not just in humans but in many animals. He begins by telling us about a small bird pecking up seed from the path; it needs both types of attention to achieve this feat without being eaten itself. It needs a narrow, focused attention in order to locate the seed on the path, to move the beak towards this seed and to pick it up in this beak before swallowing it. This involves small analytic movements focused in a limited area. The other kind of attention it needs is a much wider focus, scanning the whole sky above it and the garden around it looking for predators, which may be currently engaged in their own more focused attention in order to swoop down or pounce on the bird for their own nourishment. Humans, as you would expect, have developed both these kinds of attention in a considerably more sophisticated fashion.

The first kind we shall call 'analytic' attention. McGilchrist associates this primarily with the left side of the brain. (Others have suggested that the left–right scheme is more nuanced than in my explanation here, but I will go with McGilchrist for the purposes of this book.) This left-brain attention is the kind we use for breaking down the bigger picture into its component parts, focusing on the small details, analysing them and finding solutions to problems. The problems are defined as 'situations that are not how I want them to be' (or 'discrepancy-based processing' again). This kind of attention is extremely important to humans (and other animals) and we have achieved extraordinary feats by exploiting this to the full. However, as we have already noted, all sorts of problems in life either cannot be solved by using this type of attention or just cannot be solved at all. So, the left-brain attention is associated with the many stresses that build up in our lives as we try to fix things that cannot be fixed – or not in this way.

The other kind of attention, which McGilchrist associates with the right side of the brain, we shall call 'holistic', as it generally involves holding the whole picture in awareness rather than seeing the component parts. This kind of attention is not concerned with trying to solve, change or fix anything; it is more about coming to know the object of our attention intuitively and seeing it in its widest context. This chimes interestingly with descriptions by Oliver Sachs, in *The Man who Mistook his Wife for a Hat*, of patients with damage to the right side of their brains.[26] One man could describe every detail of the face of the man standing in front of him but could not tell that it was his own brother. Another could examine very carefully an object made of soft leather that had one bulky section about the size of the palm of his hand and then separated into five compartments each the length of a finger, but he could not recognize it as a glove.

McGilchrist's thesis is that the two sides of the brain should work in a complementary fashion, with the right brain holding the whole picture in mind but delegating the task of analysis and problem-solving relating to small parts of the picture to the left brain. The tragedy, for Western society in particular, he suggests, is that the left brain has risen above its station and thinks that its role has priority; it is so busy influencing the whole of our culture to occupy ourselves with analysis, sorting and fixing that it has no sense of what it is doing it all for, or of the big picture it is contributing to. Does this sound familiar? We read more and more reports of increasing workload, stress and depression in our culture – people working harder and harder but never seeming actually to get anywhere or to be aware of the meaning and purpose behind all their efforts.

Thomas Merton was saying something similar when he noted that humanity has now become so clever that it could blow up the whole world several times over, but that its perspective on that whole world has become so diminished that it might even do it!

What is desperately needed, then, is the reassertion of the right brain, or for this 'holistic' attention to have priority again. The big picture needs reasserting once more so that the extremely effective exploits of the left brain, through its analytic attention, can be properly brought back into the service of the whole.

Mindfulness practice steers us towards and gives us ways of practising this kind of 'holistic' attention. As noted at various points in this book, our analytic mind is very quick to try and take over. It seems that the moment it recognizes a space being opened up it can't bear this to happen, so it rushes in to fill it. But what we are trying to cultivate is that open, non-judging or loving attention that simply seeks to gaze and perceive – to recognize the object's intrinsic value as a whole without the need to analyse, interpret, set it within our own narrative and imagine the ways it could better serve us if it were different. The holistic gaze is one of love: of allowing to be, of creating space for something to come into its fullness, of holding the gaze until a fuller, deeper understanding emerges, and then of delighting in what is perceived and setting it free to be entirely itself. It may turn out to be a good thing to change things, using left-brain attention; but not until the situation/object/person has been truly appreciated and loved for what it is.

How I long to be loved like that! How I long to love like that! As noted in Chapter 4, this is the nature of divine love and it is the most precious love of all. And this, too, is the heart of prayer.

Contemplatives have always known this – that true prayer is about sitting before God in loving attention. This is what leads the Christian mystic from understanding God (which, of course, can never be achieved) to knowing or being at one with God. And my suggestion is that this is at the heart of all Christian prayer, which is why mindfulness practice can have such a central role.

It does so basically because this kind of attention makes space for God, which is what prayer and worship should be about. It is terribly tempting to approach prayer or worship with our own agenda – what we want to achieve or understand – instead of simply creating space for the Other, the divine, and to allow ourselves to be transformed by being held, in turn, in the divine gaze. Let us look at some specific forms of prayer to see where all this might fit in.

How about Bible devotion? Well, I can quote more than one of my course participants who say that they now practise mindfulness for 15 minutes then follow this with Bible study, and they find that the Bible study seems to flow much better as a result. There are a couple of reasons for this. First, quite simply, they are better able to concentrate on the passage, avoiding the usual experience of the mind wandering off to think about what their plans are for the rest of the day. Fifteen minutes of focus on the breath, noticing where the mind has drifted to, letting the thoughts go, and coming back to the breath, lays the foundations for being able to be more present when we come to Scripture. Second, it is the holistic kind of attention described here that affords greater respect and open-ness to God as we read the Bible. I would want to affirm that critical scholarship is extremely important in our interpretation of the Bible. But having done this – or read the commentary – what we need more of is the ability simply to sit with the text and allow ourselves to perceive the divine presence within it, not imposing our own agenda but being open to whatever might emerge for us.

For many people the Daily Office and recitation of psalms is their staple diet. The same could apply as for Bible study – 15 minutes of mindfulness practice immediately beforehand can make a huge difference to how present I am during the Office itself. It is not a perfect antidote, and I still find my mind wandering while saying the Office even though it is filled with words. When this happens I simply treat it as a mindfulness practice, but instead of the breath being my focus, now the words on the page are. My mind drifts, I notice it has drifted, I come back to this word on this page – the words themselves constantly bring me back to the present moment. If it is said more than once a day the Office can be treated as a means by which we keep coming back to our senses, to ourselves, to our God, throughout the day – it can be a way of waking up and returning to the present moment.

What about intercessory prayer? We may be tempted to reel off a list of people and situations we want God to bless, fix or change in some way, but this has never seemed very meaningful to me. Notably it succumbs to the temptation to keep ourselves out of the picture altogether: 'Here you are, God, this is the situation – *you* fix it!' I know I can't fix it myself, but should I have some greater part to play than simply calling things to God's attention (when God probably knows anyway – being God and all that)? I prefer the idea of holding the person or situation in the kind of loving, open-hearted, non-judging attention I have described. This expresses from the deepest part of my soul what I long for, for the person – that they might know they are held in the divine gaze of love, and also know the freedom to blossom and grow into wholeness. Let me hold back from giving God a list of things to do for this person, which are probably corrupted by my own agenda for them anyway; let me just hold them in this space of love and freedom and longing. And then see what happens.

Sometimes I come to prayer wanting to talk to God about a difficult situation I am facing. Perhaps I go for a walk and just start chatting away. This can be helpful since talking with a sense of God with me on the walk can help to clarify things. But on occasion this can get me in knots or send me round in circles. Perhaps the Scriptures are not clear or have nothing to say about this situation, and there are different voices each expressing its own way of looking at it, all present in my head vying for attention. At these times, trying to bring myself to holistic mindful attention is more fruitful. It's a bit like the 'being with the difficult' practice we looked at in Chapter 10. I bring the issue to mind but deliberately stop attempting to fix it or solve it for myself, but rather try to bring that open, holistic attentiveness to it. I step back and simply allow the situation to be in this space I have opened up and into which I invite God – not, mind you, so that God will solve it for me, but more so that we can simply look at it together.

God should not be treated as one who simply has the answers, but can be invited in as the presence of pure unjudging love. This is what transforms. We may need to be patient – it may not be solved in one go. A good practice is to step back and notice how I am responding to the situation: what thoughts are around for me, what mood does it create, are there any body sensations I can explore that might help me to be more aware of what this situation is about for me? All this awareness may be a crucial part of the picture. Another question is: 'Can I see this situation in a much wider context? Have I focused down too narrowly on this one small part of the whole, and is that why I can't see a way through?' In other words, 'Can I start to see it from God's perspective rather than just my own?' We need patience with this approach, as it may take time; that is not because God is slow – but because we are!

The use of icons in prayer would be consistent with mindfulness; we can simply gaze for a period of time on some aspect of the divine, putting aside all words and ideas and bringing that holistic attention to the image in front of us.

Finally, and inadequately in only a few lines, could we even see the Eucharist as a means by which we can invite a whole group to be drawn to that same still centre of mindful awareness? We start scattered as a people and are gradually 'gathered', first in our bodies (by arriving in the church) and then in our minds (through focusing on the word of God). We are then drawn towards the still centre beyond words, images and thoughts through focus on one tiny piece of bread and one small sip of wine, before the attention is opened up once again to a holistic awareness of the world we are sent out to serve. Is the Eucharist, then, a work of bringing people to a mindful awareness of both themselves and their God? Could this be seen as our communal weekly 'waking up'? This will need another book to explore, though!

I posed the question at the beginning of this chapter whether or not mindfulness is prayer and I recognized it as a dilemma.

I want to view it as separate so that it can be seen to be offering something to Christian prayer. But there is a fuller picture, of course, which in the end will make more sense – and that is that it is impossible to separate the two. You can't just keep God out of mindfulness! Indeed, anything done in the presence of and dedicated to God surely is prayer. So, for many of us, it is quite possible that our mindfulness practice may become our prayer – but just let's make sure we understand what mindfulness is in itself before we collapse the two.

13

Practising love

————•◦•————

I have talked about the nature of pure love, but what about actually loving people in practice? Jesus had plenty to say about this. 'The second [greatest commandment] is this, "You shall love your neighbour as yourself"' (Mark 12.31). 'You have heard that it was said, "You shall love your neighbour and hate your enemy." But I say to you, Love your enemies and pray for those who persecute you' (Matthew 5.43–44). 'This is my commandment, that you love one another as I have loved you' (John 15.12).

So, no pressure then! Fairly simple commandments that all of us should be able to aspire to with a little application! Well, some mornings maybe, when I have slept well, the day ahead of me looks rosy and the coffee is strong, I may feel generous and caring and genuinely want the best for others. Until, of course, something goes wrong and my mood dips, and then I am on the slippery slope – it is all being about me again and about what I need out of life and out of you. At least this is self-love, then? Or is it self-indulgence and self-pity? Oh dear!

I would really like to be one of those people for whom it all seems so natural: genuine, caring, selfless, always ready to respond to the needs of others. How did they get to be like that, I often wonder. Did they have a more stable upbringing than me? Is it in the genes? Or have they found some way of being better Christians? Perhaps their devotional life is more committed and so more effective?

Here is one of the great dilemmas of the Christian. We know (as does everyone else) that we are called to love, but to be honest we find we are no better at it than anyone else – and, it appears, actually worse than many who do not appear to have a life of faith or spirituality. So what is going on here?

Well, when I first turned consciously towards Christ in my life, it was in response to a great outpouring of love, which then translated into an outpouring of love, towards others around me – especially among those who had shared the same experience. But it is the ongoing development of love I am talking about. Where do we go from here?

Two aspects of mindfulness practice seem to be relevant. The first, though not specific to mindfulness, is the resolving of inner conflicts, referred to as 'inner healing' in Chapter 11. As I continue deliberately to create space to allow these conflicts to come to the surface, and open them up to the love and healing of the Holy Spirit, the natural result seems to be that I have more space available for others and am better able to show love.

There is also a specific mindfulness practice we can turn to, which I touched on very briefly in Chapter 1. This is the third of the three kinds of practice we call 'Kindness' practice. In the last few chapters I haven't suggested that you actually try the practices discussed, as they tend to rely on groundwork having been done in the early stages of the programme. But this practice could possibly be tried whether or not you have a background in mindfulness. It goes something like this:

Kindness practice

Find a place to sit where you can be alone for about 20 minutes. Begin by bringing your attention to the breath, as we have done in other practices. Then, at a moment of your choosing (I was going to say, 'when you feel settled', but sometimes this never seems to happen, so 'at a moment of your choosing' seems more realistic!), imagine yourself sitting here in this chair just for a moment. And as you hold this image of yourself in your chair, say these words as if you were wishing them for yourself:

MAY I BE SAFE AND PROTECTED.
MAY I BE AT PEACE IN MIND AND IN BODY.
MAY I LIVE WITH EASE AND WITH KINDNESS.

Say these words for yourself several times, over and over, gently and with a sense of space around them so that you become aware of how it feels to be saying these phrases for yourself. If the mind starts to wander on to other things, then, as ever, just take note of this and come back to saying the phrases – not in a mechanical way but in an open, see-how-this-feels way. Is it possible to receive these words as a kind of blessing? How does this feel? What thoughts or images emerge for us?

After a while and at a moment of your choosing, let go of the image of yourself in your awareness and bring to mind someone you might regard as a benefactor – someone who has been kind to you and towards whom you have only (or mostly) positive feelings. Then say these phrases with this person in mind, repeating them over and over, as before. This is not a race to repeat the phrases as many times as possible; once again, it is about awareness: putting something of our heart into the phrases but then being aware of what comes up for us. After a while, let go of this person in the mind's eye.

Next, bring to mind someone you might consider a neutral person in your life – someone you have neither positive nor negative feelings towards – perhaps someone you hardly know and so have not had a chance to develop any significant feelings for: a colleague who works the other side of the office from you; a commuter you see every day on the bus; the owner of the corner store. Say these same phrases for this person.

Then bring to mind someone you have some difficulty with. Perhaps not, at first, the most difficult person in your life – save that person for when you have developed this practice a bit! Rather, choose an individual who causes you some trouble or with whom you have unresolved issues. Repeat these same phrases for this person. And notice how this feels. What do you notice in yourself when saying these phrases for someone who may have hurt you?

Finally, let go of this person and bring to mind a larger group of people, perhaps your church congregation, your town, or even, if this seems possible, 'all beings'. Say these phrases for the widest group you find yourself able to imagine.

How did you get on? There is a great deal to reflect on here, including some very specific issues that come up with Christian groups.

The principle is that if love is a realistic command there must be something I can actually do to respond to it. It is no good waiting for my fluctuating feelings to fall in with the idea of love, as this may either never happen or not at the moment that I need it to. People need love when they need love, not when I feel like loving them. So, is it possible to cultivate an attitude of love within myself, towards first myself and then others around me, which might make me more likely to do something loving when the time comes? Well, this is the claim behind this practice, and many have said that it does genuinely seem to work.

People's responses to having a go at this practice are as varied as they are interesting. First up is the struggle – especially for Christians, it seems – of saying these phrases for ourselves. It is so ingrained in many of us that we should not love ourselves, that we should always put others first, that we feel a certain amount of guilt emerging as we engage with this part of the practice. One participant said she coped with it by ignoring my guidance altogether at this point in the practice and going straight to the second part! Proper self-love is crucial, though – we can't offer to another what we haven't learned to receive for ourselves, and Jesus did say to love others *as we love ourselves*. But we must not underestimate how difficult this is for many of us. And so, although I suggest it is a crucial part, it may not be the place to begin. Start where you can – where you really can sense love within you rather than trying to battle with your own self-hatred. Some have even suggested that we could begin by bringing to mind a beloved pet! If that stirs love within you, then that could well be the place to start. I think it was Augustine who said (though it might have been Bob Marley!): there is only one love. So whatever you identify as your way in to cultivating an attitude of love, start there – it is the same love.

Another area people get stuck in – more obviously – is the person who causes you problems. Some make the mistake of beginning with too difficult a person, and get overwhelmed with their own feelings of anger or hatred, which is why it is best to start with a less difficult individual until we have developed this practice a bit. One man said he could not think of anyone he knew so he brought to mind his most hated politician! But this was equally difficult because he honestly felt he did not wish any good things for this person. This really surprised him, but at least it was an awareness that helped him realize what he was working with within himself. The intention here, though, is not to *feel* nice feelings, for such feelings may not come. Rather it is to practise 'inclining the mind' towards a more friendly attitude.

Jesus said we should love our enemies, though, and many participants, especially those who approach this practice gently, building up slowly from those they find it easier to wish well, clearly find that this has made a big difference to how they engage with people who are difficult for them on an ongoing basis. They may not end up liking the individuals concerned but the testimony has been that somehow things have changed. One or two have told me how they made their difficult boss or work colleague the focus of this practice and then found their own attitudes gradually changing. The situation itself did not necessarily change, nor did the boss, but their own anger or tension was somewhat released, which set that whole situation in a different context.

I have practised saying these phrases for those attending a meeting I am about to go into, especially if I am expecting it to be a tense encounter. I say them for the participants of my mindfulness class, particularly when I am plagued by thoughts about the inadequacy of my own teaching skills. I find that this puts me in touch with the compassion within me – which turns out to be just as valuable as well-honed technical skills.

One question that comes up with groups of Christians is: 'How does this relate to intercessory prayer?' Who am I asking to bring this protection, safety and peace to the person I have in my mind?' In other words, what part does God play in this? Well, when mindfulness is taught in non-religious (or Buddhist) contexts, God is not part of the picture at all. We are not asking any being actually to do anything for us; we are finding this is an effective way of developing a genuine attitude of kindness within ourselves towards others. Nothing may change in the other, but I change. A change in me might be the very thing that leads to change in the other through, say, an improvement in the whole atmosphere, but it is not my aim to change the other; it is to allow a change to happen in me. Neuroscientists will concur about the effectiveness of this practice, by telling us how closely linked the hearing mechanisms in the brain are with those that lead to action. It is another way of helping us to shift from the analytical, task-focused 'doing' mode of the mind to the 'being' mode, which is where compassion is found.

But this is still all about the one who is saying the phrases. For Christians, who recognize the presence of the divine in all things, it is best to see it as another way of opening ourselves up to the work of the Holy Spirit within us. If God is within us, then love is within us – it's just that we tend to get rather out of touch with this love when we are stressed, hurt or angry. This practice is a means by which we open up the channels of love within ourselves and connect with the divine compassion within. And this, of course, can be the beginning of other changes that we may long for or pray for. 'Be the change you want to see in the world,' said Gandhi. So it starts with us but it does not end there.

The phrases used needn't be the ones I have suggested. Or, once you have used these phrases for a while, try out others that might have particular resonances for you. And noting, as we have, that proper self-love is a key part of the picture, the following is a version of this practice that may help to take us deeper into the business of developing an appropriate attitude of kindness and generosity towards ourselves.

Practising self-love

This practice could well begin with calling to mind our all-loving God, and considering the question, 'What is it that God most longs for, for me?' The development of the phrases below are based on my own sense of God's love for me. You may like to consider how you would answer this question and develop the phrases you would use for yourself.

Start by focusing on the breath. Then, as before, imagine yourself sitting here – hold an image of yourself in your mind's eye. Then begin saying the phrases, just for yourself; then reflect on the way I have developed them; finally reflect on the phrases you might choose for yourself in each section.

May I be safe and protected. May I be free from danger or the threat of danger; may that which is vulnerable and precious in me be kept safe – not violated; may I know a safe space where I can roam free, explore, pick easy fruit and bask in the sun; may I . . .

May I be at peace in mind. May I be happy and contented as far as is possible; may I be full of joy and liberated – free to become who I am; may my energies flow and mental health remain good – flourishing; when I am low may there be someone there for me; may I . . .

May I be at peace in my body. May I be as healthy as is possible for me; may I be well and stay well; may I be free from pain as far as is possible; may I be able to be with the pain that remains without fear, anger or tension; may I . . .

May I live with ease and with kindness. May I live with as little stress as possible; may there be space in and around my days; may there be kindness, warmth and generosity flowing in my relationships; may I see beauty every day; may I . . .

Finally, return to the breath once again before finishing the practice.

14

Reconnecting with nature

————•◦•————

Up to now, all my chapter headings have been what I assume are familiar themes. The idea has been to pick up on aspects of faith that most Christians will recognize as something they aspire to or to which they acknowledge that we are called as Christians. I do not make the same assumption for this chapter, as it is relatively recently that the Christian ecological agenda has become prominent.

Let me start by reflecting on how this is just as crucial a part of our calling as other topics I have covered. Picking up on the theme of God's unity explored in Chapter 4, the story runs, in brief, like this. God is one, and everything that there is is one in God. Human beings have, though, both in our minds and in our practice, caused what should be united instead to be divided. We are divided from our selves through guilt and shame; we are divided from one another through fear and greed; and we have divided ourselves from the rest of nature in order to be able to exploit nature for our own ends with no real awareness, until relatively recently, of the consequences of this. However, we are now beginning to become more fully aware of how our exploitation of the natural world is damaging not just the habitat of many, many species on the planet but also our own habitat.

One of the reasons we have been blind to this is the separation we have set up in our minds between us and the rest of nature. Either we have misunderstood the implications of God's words to the archetypal first humans, Adam and Eve (the famous 'have *dominion* over' in Genesis 1.28), or the writer has misunderstood God, but it seems to me that it all went wrong when Adam and Eve decided that pretty much anything in the garden was for them, and that they could take what they wanted, whenever they wanted. In other words, with the eating of the apple, in their minds they were subscribing to a utilitarian view of nature and an anthropocentric view at that: it is all there *for us*. And so the third fundamental separation happened: humans and nature were two separate entities, and humans were superior. So, whenever the needs of humans and the needs of nature clashed, it would be those of humans that would take priority.

The alternative view is that humans are *part* of nature and that every time we diminish nature, we diminish ourselves as well. St Paul recognized this fundamental principle in relation to the Christian community in 1 Corinthians 12.26: 'If one member suffers, all suffer together with it.' But we now need to realize that it is true of all of nature too. Humans and the rest of nature are part of one creation and all part of an extraordinarily balanced ecosystem. We will survive together or not at all.

Now, of course, recycling, reduction in energy costs and outlawing the use of fossil fuels are all very much part of the agenda. But you can't help but feel the half-heartedness of our commitment here, much of the time. If our efforts to show greater respect to the planet take extra energy, extra time, cost more or risk my own country's short-term economy and so lose me votes, then I will hesitate – *unless* I have experienced this reconnection with nature at a deep level within me. If we can come to speak, with St Francis, of brother son and sister moon, of sister birds, flowers, trees and rivers, if these could become as much part of our own family as the other Christians Paul talks about in 1 Corinthians – then maybe we might start to make real sacrifices for the sake of the survival of all of God's creation.

But how does this happen? How does this connection at the level of the heart begin to take place?

Since early on in my teaching of mindfulness I have included an element of mindfulness in nature. The principle is simple. It is about bringing the same quality of open-hearted, non-judging, holistic attention to nature that we bring to our breath, to our bodies, to sounds and to our thoughts. Here is a simple practice:

Mindfulness in nature

Go out into the garden if you have one, or into the park or the woods. If there is no green space near you, try using a house plant. Choose a single flower or plant and sit down really close to it. Now, just look. No need to know what its name is or anything about this plant or flower – in fact, this practice is easier if you don't. All you are seeking to do is to pay really careful attention to the colours, the shapes and the patterns of the flower. You may have seen many of these before but never at this moment of this day and in the particular mood state you are in now. So this is a unique, once-in-a-lifetime experience. So see if it is possible to bring the same sort of curiosity we brought to the raisin we looked at in Chapter 1. What do you see? Keep looking. What else do you see? Where is your mind wandering to? How this would look good in the house or might be good to eat; how this compares with other similar plants or flowers; how you could be getting on with something more useful right now? Notice the thoughts and keep coming back to the flower. Is it possible to bring to this flower that sense of loving attention that speaks of our recognition of its intrinsic value? Once again, notice how quickly our minds want to create narrative, to analyse or to see everything as a problem to be solved or as something we like or don't like – all referencing me as the centre of it all. This sort of attention brings the recognition that this flower is not here for me but is just here. Let me gaze on the extraordinary beauty that I see and accord it its true value.

Finally, you could try using a version of the kindness practice introduced in the last chapter by saying these phrases:

MAY THIS FLOWER BE SAFE AND PROTECTED.
MAY THIS FLOWER BE TREATED WITH RESPECT
AND WITH KINDNESS.
MAY THIS FLOWER FIND SPACE TO GROW AND
TO FLOURISH.

When I was first invited to do an activity similar to this I was staying with a community that was founded around the recognition of the true value of nature and now it was part of their life and lifestyle. We were invited to walk along a beautiful river valley and just to 'listen' to nature around us. It seemed very simple, but it turned out to be a profound experience for me. It was the huge rocks of the riverbed that I became most fully aware of; I was struck by the realization that these boulders had been there for thousands of years before I came along, and would continue to be there for thousands if not millions of years after I had departed. No way had they been put there for me! Instead I was but a fleeting moment in their own history. I felt a deep sense of awe and respect. I began to recognize my place in the order of things.

There is a view that asks, 'Why would you protect what you have not yet learned to love?' As we reflected in Chapter 13, love needs cultivating and there are ways of doing this.

You may have heard of the Forest Church movement. It has been described as 'forest school for grown-ups', though, significantly, with a spiritual element. There are now Forest Churches all over the country, each with different characteristics. A couple of years ago I was involved in setting up the Oxford Forest Church.

Its aim is simply to go about this business of reconnecting humans with the rest of nature in an intentional way. Our gatherings, currently six a year, are very simple and follow a broadly eucharistic structure.

We gather in some chosen landscape venue, sometimes sing songs or read poems, and tell each other how we are if we choose. We reflect on this particular landscape and the natural species around us, as well as the particular point in the cycle of the season. We then go off on our own for about 30 minutes specifically in order to bring this kind of mindful attention to what we see, hear, smell, feel and possibly taste. We might find a place to sit or we might walk slowly. It is not really a nature walk as such because we are putting aside thoughts of what we like or don't like or what we may know or not know. Instead we are just seeing shapes and colours; just hearing sounds; just feeling textures; just smelling smells. We are seeking to allow nature to be what it is and where it is and perhaps to perceive our own place in the midst. We may also become aware of ourselves as we walk along, but again not drifting off into our normal endless train of thought that can take us anywhere and fast. Simply noticing what appears to be present in me – reactions to what I see; memories stirred; mood changes – I pay the same kind of attention to myself as I do to the nature around me because I am part of nature too. I am connected. I too am here. We are here together. There is a mutual respect – a sense of belonging to one another, a sense of being at home with one another.

When we gather again at a prearranged time and place we share food, possibly sing again and share, if we choose, something of our experiences, just as we do in class after a mindfulness practice. And, of course, no experience is either right or wrong. The only objective is to develop the art of noticing, of awareness – this time of our own connectedness to nature.

As with all mindfulness practices, actual changes to my life come gradually, as I keep practising. So I need to practise for the sake of practice itself rather than because of a particular outcome. In my case the small changes I have noticed in my own life do seem significant. Now when I turn a light off in the house it does not feel like a duty. Nor does it come ladled with annoyance at whoever left it on (or not much). When I flick the switch I experience more of a sense of love for the nature I am learning to protect. I have renewed commitment to follow an eco-agenda in my church and local area. It is a slow process, but I would like to think I am adjusting my lifestyle a little at a time. I consider more carefully what means of transport I choose, use less paper and aim to eat more vegetarian food. What I am trying to say is that such practice of mindfulness in nature will not be a miracle cure for the world's ecological woes. But I believe it has a part to play, and in the meantime Forest Church is a beautiful, cheap and soul-quenching activity on a Saturday afternoon!

15
Daily living

———————

It has often been a criticism of religion, and especially of those who dare to take it seriously and do things like pray, go on retreat and read the Bible avidly, that this might be all very well for them but how is it helping with anything in the world? There are always stories around of people who spend all day meditating in their room but don't lift a finger to help with the chores. Nice peaceful feelings inside, maybe, but no use to anyone else. In other words, the same age-old criticism of Mary as compared with Martha, but actually often quite justified. Jesus was, at other points, very strong on this: 'Not everyone who says to me "Lord, Lord", will enter the kingdom of heaven, but only one who does the will of my Father in heaven' (Matthew 7.21).

So, in the spirit of the best of the Christian tradition, which emphasizes the integral connection between the inner and the outer life – and that there really is only one life – mindfulness is not primarily about becoming good at mindfulness practice but, rather, about becoming a more mindful person in daily life.

I was much encouraged in this when I was on retreat once. I have never found mindfulness practice easy, and when I go on retreat this is doubly apparent. The usual opening question by the leader when you go for a private conversation is: 'So, how are you getting on?' To which my usual initial response (as I related previously) is, 'Terrible!' My mind has been all over the place; all the things that really stress me have crowded in because there is so little to distract me from them; my back is aching through so much sitting; and so on. This particular retreat leader really helped me by saying that there are some people who seem to have a blissful time on retreat but it makes no difference to their lives at home, while others have a really hard time on retreat but find things have really shifted in them when they go back to their daily lives. 'Much better to be in the second category,' he said simply. Even better, I am thinking, to be in the category of those who are changed for the better *and* have wonderful times on retreat! But I know he was just responding to where I was at the time.

Some people have asked me, rather despairingly, whether it gets any easier – whether, after a few years of practice, I am 'better' at keeping my concentration on my breath for longer. My answer to this is 'not really'. But I can say that I have seen the change in my daily life. I become aware more easily and more quickly when I am in a dangerous mood; I am better at not sending emails in the heat of the moment; I am more able to stop and become aware of how what you have just said has made me feel before responding; I am more aware of myself drifting towards a narrow, blinkered approach to my work – before it is too late; I am better at remembering that the person I feel hurt by has their own perspective on the situation; I am much better at managing stress; I get fewer and shorter periods of depression; and my wife says I am less defensive! It's not how good I am at practising that counts. It's the effect it has on my life.

Built into the mindfulness course, particularly the course based on the *Frantic World* book, are some practices deliberately designed to make these sorts of connections and to bring mindfulness into daily life. In the book they are called 'habit releasers'. These are great because they are a way of playing with mindfulness and having a bit of fun, and there is plenty of space for us to be creative. They are based on the principle that there are many activities we do habitually in life. When something becomes a routine this may seem comforting and give a sense of security, but it also means we stop noticing – because there is nothing to notice; we have seen it all before. If you visit someone who lives near a busy road or motorway (assuming you don't), that person hardly notices the traffic sounds that might really annoy you. After a while, we just tune out to what is there all the time – we become unaware of it.

So the 'habit releaser' is for a daily activity that you might normally do in one particular way; now you choose to change perhaps one small aspect of it. Then you observe what you become aware of as a result. What new things did I notice? How did it feel? What was my experience that time? How did the world look or feel to me when I did it this way? The results may not be earth-shattering in themselves, but what we are seeking to encourage is the habit of awareness. And actually just simple things, when we become aware of them, can turn out to be some of the great delights in our day.

Here are a few examples from the *Frantic World* book:

- Try going to work by a different route or a different mode of transport.
- Have one meal a week in silence with no reading, no radio or TV on – and focus on just eating.
- Instead of turning on the radio or TV when you get in, check the listings and choose one programme to watch or listen to – and then turn it off!
- If you always sit in the same chair at home, at meetings or in church – sit in a different one.
- (This is a tough one.) Meet a friend at the cinema at a pre-arranged time, having not checked the listings, and go to the first film that starts after you have arrived.

It might be interesting to try one of these – or all of them – and then make up your own. You don't have to like doing things a different way but what can happen is that this may wake us up to things we hadn't previously been aware of. Most of all, it reawakens our senses to things going on around us all the time, so many of which we had stopped noticing because of the routines we fall into.

Another practice from the Mindfulness Based Cognitive Therapy course designed to bring mindfulness into the middle of our day is the 'three-minute breathing space'. It doesn't necessarily have to be exactly three minutes, but its brevity is what makes it possible to do at any point during the day. We have noted throughout this book the two modes of mind in which we can find ourselves caught up. Perhaps the more familiar to us is the mode where we are focused on tasks, sorting, planning, fixing, organizing – the 'doing' mode. We have also noticed that even when we stop and simply focus on our breath, giving ourselves no tasks to do, the mind still wants to carry on sorting, fixing and planning – there is quite a strong compulsion here. Sometimes we can get so deeply caught up in this mode that we can become lost in it, achieving less and less, getting more and more stressed and gradually losing the big picture. At times like these we really need a big dose of the other mode of mind, the 'being' mode, which is able to reconnect us with the big picture by bringing us back to the present moment in an open and unjudging way.

This, I have argued, is where God will be for us – not lost in our own compulsions, caught up in our anxieties about the past or our determination to shape the future in a particular way, but open to the wider perspective of the present moment. The present moment is always where God will be, but sometimes we need to stop, look up, and make a conscious decision to make space for God. But how do we do this? How do we make the shift, in the middle of a busy day when our prayer time or mindfulness practice seems a million miles away? Monastics commit themselves to a number of short and simple acts of prayer called 'offices' at fixed times of day to keep bringing them back to their centre – to God. But we don't have the space for that in our day and, anyway, I am in the middle of a different kind of 'office' which, right now, is part of the problem.

The three-minute breathing space is not just a 'time out', a breather to give me a little break so that I can then go back to doing what I was doing before in exactly the same way. It is intended to help us actually to shift this mode of mind. For the Christian, it could literally be about letting God in.

The three-minute breathing space

Wherever you are, whatever you are doing, stop for a moment. If it is possible, adjust your posture slightly to help you to become aware of your own physical presence, which is your gateway into the present moment – where God is! Close your eyes if this is possible or comfortable.

Stage one is to allow yourself to become aware of all that is going on for you right now, in this moment: what thoughts there are around in the mind; what sort of mood state you are in; whether there are any body sensations for you to notice. Whatever is there, simply take note. You don't need to decide whether this is good or bad, but just note what is here. Do this for about a minute.

Stage two is then to shift the awareness to the breath, and if possible to a very narrow focus on one part of the body where the breath is most apparent to you: perhaps the movements of the lower abdomen or the chest. The mind may still be drifting off back to the other things it was engaged with but, as far as is possible, keep coming back to the breath. Stay with this for a minute.

Stage three is to widen the attention once again, this time to take in the whole of the body. Still be aware of the breath in the background, but now with a sense of the breath flowing through the body. Keep breathing like this for a short while, perhaps deliberately opening outwards and allowing the body to soften in its stance. In this way we are reconnecting with the body, with this moment, and making space for God.

And so we have 'woken up'. This is our 'prodigal son' moment, where we have come back to our senses, realized what is going on and invited God in to be part of things once again. And then we find that we have *choices*. We could perhaps go back to what we were doing before but with a different attitude – a new gentleness, kindness or a greater wisdom. Or we could decide we need a break or to change tasks – or even that this task is not taking us anywhere and really needs to be abandoned. Perhaps most usefully, we may suddenly realize that we are not supposed to be here at all but at a meeting that started five minutes ago!

A warning about the three-minute breathing space, though: it does actually need practice. It is not easy to get the hang of, particularly because of how compulsive the 'doing' mode is for so many of us. We normally suggest that participants practise this three times a day for a week or two before trying to bring it in at moments when they feel they really need it – times of stress or lowering of mood. The trouble is that when I am stuck in my 'doing' mode I don't *want* to stop! I want to get this done and that finished. If I stop now I will lose momentum or create other problems. This mode of mind is in charge and it likes it that way; it won't give up being in charge without a fight. So, practice is needed. But when the practice has become a natural thing for us it can be an absolutely invaluable tool to help bring mindfulness into the everyday.

You may find other creative ways to be mindful through the day without taking any extra time. I have a very short walk through a bit of woodland to my church. I don't plan things in my head as I walk but I look at the leaves or focus on the sensations in the soles of my feet. Washing up (remember the Martha and Mary exercise) is (usually!) not a chore but an opportunity to be mindful. Very often I don't take my coffee back to my desk after lunch but for a moment simply sit quietly with it – sometimes reading but better still just being quiet. This activity can take all of five minutes but it seems a very precious five minutes to me.

So, however you do it, this is the point: mindful lives – or, in Brother Lawrence's phrase, 'practising the presence of God'.[27]

Epilogue: Life in all its fullness

So, we come to the end of the book, and it is time for the most important question of all: 'What is it all for?' We have looked at what Christians feel called to believe, do and experience and how mindfulness might have a part to play in enabling these to happen. But unless we set everything in the wider context of, ultimately, what it is all for, then we will be in danger of letting our analytic, 'doing' mode of mind take over again, by merely allowing it the gleeful sense that it has something new to do! And having something new to do can be quite enlivening and motivating – for a while. But when the struggles come, the rising waves are threatening and the barriers or layers of hard rock appear, what will inspire us to keep going?

Here is an illustration that inspires me. If you like music you might decide to pick up a musical instrument and learn the skills required to play it. I play a bit of guitar so this involves scales, chord shapes and sequences, strumming patterns and so on, and it can be quite satisfying to begin to master these skills. But all this skill learning will soon lose its appeal if I lose sight of the greater purpose of what I am doing – which is to make something called 'music'! It is the holistic, right-brain awareness that puts us in touch with the big picture, and it is really important to have this firmly in our minds if we are to persevere. So, what is the 'music' we are seeking to create with mindfulness? What is the big picture that practising mindfulness is serving?

At the end of every mindfulness course we invite participants to write down, just for themselves, something that they truly value in life that might serve as a compelling reason for continuing to practise mindfulness, especially at times when it is most difficult and they least want to do it. We always tell them to keep these reasons private so that they can be as honest as possible with themselves. Thus, I have no examples to quote – except my own. Here is what I wrote after the last two courses I did as a participant:

- Because I want to open up to life, people, friends, music, pleasure!
- Because life is more than just one task after another.

They are not theological, as I was trying to engage with the ethos of the particular course I was in at the time and I thought I would just go with whatever came to my mind first. However, they both still resonate with me very powerfully, and also with some familiar words of Jesus in John 10.10: 'I came that they may have life, and have it abundantly.' As a Christian, it would seem to me not a bad overall motivation – that we are doing this in order to be more open to the abundant life that Jesus came to bring. I sometimes think there might be more 'worthy' reasons to be practising mindfulness that are more about what I might contribute to the world, but when I come back to it and try to be really honest with myself, I really do want some (or a lot) of this 'life in all its fullness', and this is a very powerful motivator for me. I would add, though, that having found it I also want to bring as many people with me as possible – or enable as many others as possible to experience it too.

What would your motivation be? Why are you reading this book? What is it that might honestly move you towards practising mindfulness – not out of duty but with passion and out of love? Perhaps it is more about others – you want to be a better mother/father or partner (it was somewhat amusing to note how many of the men who came to a recent 'Mindfulness for Men' retreat had been put on to it by their wives!). It may be to do with your mental health – perhaps with managing stress or depression. Or you may simply want to be a better follower of Christ or able to develop a deeper prayer life. Whatever your motivation, it could be well worth trying to seeing if you can connect with it in yourself now; write it down and leave it on your desk or on a noticeboard for yourself – or on your screensaver.

And all this because mindfulness is 'not just for Christmas'! It is, in my experience, a slow burner. The practices are called that for a reason. The skills we are learning come with repetition and sometimes only over a considerable period of time, so we need to be in it for the long term and we need to find ways of keeping going as the music may not come straight away. I complained to my guitar teacher recently that I got bored with practising scales even though I knew I would not gain the technique to be able to play the way I wanted to without doing these particular scales. Once he had chastised me for 'not being very mindful' (fair enough!), he suggested that I should simply start enjoying the sound of the guitar, for its own sake and not as a means to an end. 'It's a lovely guitar,' he said, 'you've spent money on it. Listen to the tone of every note.' So now I do. Scales (most of the time) are no longer something to be avoided but can be enjoyed for their own sake. I just listen to the tone.

We may need something of this attitude with mindfulness too. We need to find ways of practising that we can value just for themselves. Changes will come to our lives, but not necessarily the ones we were looking for, nor as quickly as we would like. Was it not ever so with God, though, who knows better than us both what we need and how fast we can move? So, let us practise and practise, and let us practise and practise, and let us be ever open to the adventure of life that may unfold. Or, as John O'Donohue the philosopher, priest and poet so beautifully put it:

> I would love to live like a river flows,
> carried by the surprise of its own unfolding.[28]

Notes

1 The YouTube video can be found by searching for 'Healing and the mind Jon Kabat-Zinn, Bill Moyers'.

2 M. Williams and D. Penman, *Mindfulness: A Practical Guide to Finding Peace in a Frantic World*, London: Piatkus, 2011.

3 K. Nataraja, *Journey to the Heart*, London: Canterbury Press, 2011.

4 C. Potok, *In the Beginning*, Harmondsworth: Penguin, 1975.

5 N. Lash, *Believing Three Ways in One God*, London: SCM Press, 1992.

6 C. S. Lewis, *The Four Loves*, London: Fount, 1977.

7 D. Cupitt, *Theology's Strange Return*, London: SCM Press, 2010.

8 S. Vanauken, *A Severe Mercy*, London: Hodder & Stoughton, 1977.

9 Cupitt, *Theology's Strange Return*, p. 5.

10 *The Lion King*, Walt Disney, 1994.

11 *The Matrix*, Warner Bros, 1999.

12 As suggested in the text, this is a much more nuanced debate than I have the space to go into, but here are some pointers. The more recent science of 'epigenetics' (genes that can be activated or remain dormant as a result of experiences after birth) will have somewhat complicated the idea that everything is determined by our birth genes. Two relevant articles are: 'The free will delusion', *New Scientist*, 16 April 2011, p. 32; 'New chapter opens in free will debate', *New Scientist*, 11 August 2012, p. 10.

13 J. Haidt, *The Happiness Hypothesis*, London: Arrow, 2006, chapter 1.

14 I don't think this potted history of the decentring of human consciousness is original – or not entirely – but I cannot find where I got it from. So, apologies if some of this comes from someone else's ideas.

15 'Your clever body', *New Scientist*, 15 October 2011, p. 35; 'Alimentary thinking', *New Scientist*, 15 December 2012, p. 39.

16 C. S. Lewis, *The Lion, the Witch and the Wardrobe*, London: Geoffrey Bles, 1950.

17 C. Ten Boom, *The Hiding Place*, Ada, MI: Chosen Books, 1971.
18 *A Beautiful Mind*, DreamWorks Pictures, 2001.
19 D. Tutu and M. Tutu, *The Book of Forgiving*, New York: William Collins, 2014.
20 N. Nicholson, *Shadowlands*, Samuel French, 1989.
21 Rumi, 'The Guest House', *Rumi Poems*, New York: Alfred Knopf, 2006.
22 S. Spencer, *Christ in the Wilderness*, National Gallery of Victoria, Melbourne, Australia.
23 *Crocodile Dundee*, 20th Century Fox, 1986.
24 H. Williams, *Some Day I'll Find You*, London: Fount, 1982.
25 I. McGilchrist, *The Master and His Emissary*, New Haven, CT: Yale University Press, 2009.
26 O. Sachs, *The Man who Mistook his Wife for a Hat*, London: Picador, 1985.
27 Brother Lawrence, *The Practice of the Presence of God*, London: One World, 1993.
28 Unpublished quotation.

Mindfulness courses
and further reading

Mindfulness 'self-help' courses

These are courses you can work through by reading the book at home and using the CD included, which guides you through the meditations.

A general course

M. Williams and D. Penman, *Mindfulness: A Practical Guide to Finding Peace in a Frantic World*, London: Piatkus, 2011.

For depression in particular

J. Teasdale, M. Williams and Z. Segal, *The Mindful Way Workbook*, New York: Guilford Press, 2014.

M. Williams, J. Teasdale, Z. Segal and J. Kabat-Zinn, *The Mindful Way Through Depressions*, New York: Guilford Press, 2007.

Focusing on health issues

V. Burch and D. Penman, *Mindfulness for Health: A Practical Guide to Relieving Pain, Reducing Stress and Restoring Wellbeing*, London: Piatkus, 2013.

Finding a course near you

The Oxford Mindfulness Centre has information on its website about different kinds of courses, best practice guidelines and how to find a course near you: <www.oxfordmindfulness.org>.

Further reading

The Christian contemplative tradition through the ages

K. Nataraja (ed.), *Journey to the Heart*, London: Canterbury Press, 2011.

Christian teachers on prayer, consistent with mindfulness

M. Laird, *Into the Silent Land*, London: Darton, Longman and Todd, 2006.

A. de Mello, *Awareness*, London: Fount, 1990.

Clinical books

F. Didonna (ed.), *Clinical Handbook of Mindfulness*, New York: Springer, 2009.

Z. Segal, M. Williams and J. Teasdale, *Mindfulness-based Cognitive Therapy for Depression*, New York: Guilford Press, 2013.

Mindfulness and nature

B. Stanley, *Forest Church*, Llangurig: Mystic Christ Press, 2013.

C. Thompson, *Mindfulness and the Natural World*, Lewes: Leaping Hare Press, 2013.